The
Liturgical Home

ADVENT

Ashley Tumlin Wallace

ANGLICAN
COMPASS

Cover Art and Design: Kevin Lindholm

For more resources visit
www.AshleyTumlinWallace.com

CONTENTS

FOREWORD

*A*T ANGLICAN COMPASS, we help you navigate with clarity and charity, pointing to Christ as the way, the truth, and the life.

The Church calendar is a way of life—a rhythm that's meant to form our families and our friendships. But how do we live it out on the ground, in our homes? What does The Liturgical Home look like? To answer that question, it really helps to have a good friend who can speak from experience. And Ashley is a great friend, with abundant experience from many years making a home with her husband and their four children.

In the pages that follow, let Ashley be your guide, a source of new ideas (and recipes!) for observing The Liturgical Home with family and friends. You will have a lot of fun along the way. And even more important, you will grow closer to Jesus.

PREFACE

⁓

"For everything there is a season" Ecclesiastes 3:1.

Growing up in the south, I didn't know a lot about seasons. I mean, I knew about them from books and movies, but I had never really experienced them. The only seasons we had in the Florida panhandle were kind of hot, hot, and very hot.

When my husband was given the opportunity to attend seminary in Wisconsin, we were nervous to leave our home and family but we were also excited to be making such a radical change and to experience a world filled with seasons that were completely alien to us.

The fall in Wisconsin was beyond anything we could have imagined. Brilliant reds, golds, oranges, and yellows exploded from the trees. Every scene took your breath away, every view looked like a postcard picture. Hooray for seasons! Hooray for us being wild and adventurous! Little did we know, falls in Wisconsin are short-lived and winter comes all too quickly!

In the winter of 2002, I found myself far from the life I once knew. Here I was, a beach girl transplanted to the frosty climes of Wisconsin. For those of you who have never experienced a Wisconsin winter, let me explain: you don't leave the house . . . ever! It is just too cold! Especially when you're from Florida! And seeing as how I had just given birth to my second child, we were housebound in a major way. I felt very isolated and I was left with a lot of time to think. I thought deep thoughts like, "Who am I?" "What is my purpose in the world?" and the much more desperate, **"WHAT IN THE WORLD AM I DOING IN WISCONSIN?"**

The days were so long and cold. It felt like I did the same thing every day. There seemed to be very little structure to my life and my days felt monotonous and without form. We were Christians so we read Bible stories to our children, we talked to them about Jesus and we sang Christian songs with them but that filled up a very small portion of the day. It just didn't seem like enough to me. I wanted a lot more meaning in my day. I had a deep desire to incorporate the things of God more in my life. I wanted my everyday life to be permeated with the Spirit of the living God.

One night as I was reading a local magazine, I was drawn to an interview with a new chef from a restaurant in nearby Milwaukee. He was describing the foods that he was currently serving. They were all traditional Advent foods from his small village in France. I was so intrigued. I had no idea that other countries, other cultures had particular foods that they made for Advent and Christmas.

A chef who was preparing traditional Advent foods from his village in France? I wondered how many more traditions do other cultures have? How many other ways have people celebrated the seasons of the church? I wanted to find out more.

This was an entirely new concept to me that a whole region could be so shaped by the traditions of their faith. I loved it. I started asking a lot of questions and doing a lot of research.

This whole world opened up to me - a world of possibilities. People around the world were living out their faith with traditions that were similar but with regional and ethnic differences based on foods and geographic regions. It reminded me of St. Paul's analogy about the body of Christ in 1 Corinthians. We are all uniquely made and yet we are all one body of Christ.

I began to think about my own little family. Who are we as a family within the larger framework of Christians? What traditions do I want to embrace? I began to get so excited. What if my day could ebb and flow with the greater life of the church? What if my day could be filled with meaning, richness, color, taste . . . things that involve all of our senses? What if I could create an atmosphere of faith in my home, traditions that enriched and gave structure, purpose and unity with the local church and then the wider, worldwide church? Themes of wholeness and identity began to take shape in my heart.

I started researching and collecting traditions from all over the world. I compiled them all and I incorporated these traditions into my own family. During Advent, the Advent wreath is dressed in evergreen boughs that my children bring in from the woods. We place it on the dining room table and every Sunday we sit down in the darkness, light the Advent candles and learn anew the story of our salvation. As I look around, the light of the candles casts a soft glow and every face is filled with a sense of wonder. This is what celebrating Advent does, it takes the chaos and the frantic rush of our lives and it forces us to slow down. We are given, as a family, time to prepare our hearts for the coming of Christ so that when Christmas finally arrives, we greet the day with true joy.

What you hold in your hand is the result of my personal journey through the seasons of the Church. I hope it will bless you as a resource and as a guide through your own journey. Here's to embracing all that the seasons of the Church have to offer!

Truly,

Ashley Wallace

HOW TO USE THIS BOOK

*I*n the Liturgical Home you will encounter beautiful traditions and celebrations from all over the world. I hope it will bless you on your journey through the seasons of the Church.

WHAT ARE THE SEASONS OF THE CHURCH?

For those who are new to liturgical living, we have included a brief introduction to the seasons of the Church.

WHAT IS ADVENT?

In this chapter you will be introduced to the season of Advent and the traditional ways it has been celebrated around the world.

HOW TO CELEBRATE ADVENT

Because the way our culture gets ready for Christmas is quite different from the way the Church celebrates Advent, we've included some suggestions about how to prepare ourselves, as individuals and as families, for Advent.

ADVENT TRADITIONS FOR THE ENTIRE SEASON

Some Advent traditions, such as the Advent Calendar and Advent Wreath, last for the entire season. This section contains ideas to celebrate Advent that apply to the whole season.

ADVENT TRADITIONS FOR SPECIFIC DAYS

Other Advent traditions, such as celebrating the Feast of St. Nicholas (December 6) or the "O Antiphons" (December 17–23), only apply to specific days. Check this section for Advent traditions for particular days.

Remember that none of these Advent ideas are mandates. Be realistic in your selections. Choose observances that seem interesting and manageable. It is not necessary to do all of them. The ideas are not meant to be a burden or to cause stress. They are meant to be a blessing to you and way to unify you with your friends, your family, your church, and the church universal as we move through the seasons of the Church.

ADVENT DEVOTIONS

We have included devotions at the end of each of the special days in this book. It is our hope that these devotions will help to guide you in prayer. They have been designed to be easy to use and understand. Decide on the right time to have a devotion. Right before or after dinner or before bed will often be the best time.

If you have more than one person participating in the devotions, invite different members to be the leader, to read the readings, or to light the candles. In families it can be fun to allow the children to lead the devotions from time to time.

ADVENT RECIPES

Sugar cookies are just the beginning! Although sweets are traditionally off-limits during Advent, there are plenty of special days where culinary delights are allowed and encouraged! This section will teach you how to make everything from Speculatius to Lebkuchen.

WHAT ARE THE SEASONS OF THE CHURCH?

*T*he faith of God's people, throughout the history of Israel and the Church, has been a holistic faith. It was a faith that encompassed all areas of the people's lives and that ebbed and flowed with the changing of the seasons. Their faith was individual, but just as important, it was a corporate faith. Everyone celebrated the same festivals and rituals together and this gave them a sense of belonging to something bigger than themselves. Theirs was also an experiential faith that involved all of their senses with the use of incense, the eating and abstaining from certain foods, the hearing and teaching of the Word of God, and the singing of spiritual songs.

It was in this way that, for the Jewish people, time became much more than just what the Greeks called *chronos* – the passing of time as a measurable quantity of days and weeks and years. Celebrating the festivals and rituals of their faith sanctified the *chronos* of their lives and made it *kairos*. This is time that is not measured by its duration, but instead by its quality and significance. The festivals and rituals reminded them daily that they had been chosen by God to be his people and that it was their relationship with him, and nothing else, that gave their lives significance.

When the long-awaited Messiah finally came in the person of Jesus everything changed for those who believed in him. The old festivals told only the first part of the story. Now a new *kairos* had dawned and new celebrations were necessary. The creation of the Seasons of the Church, the liturgical calendar that begins each year with the First Sunday of Advent, was the natural and beautiful response to the coming of the Messiah. He was the fulfillment of Holy Scripture and the consummation of all hopes and desires. The Church experienced Christ's resurrection as the ultimate fulfillment of all things promised by God and so new celebrations were created.

The earliest record we have of what would later develop into the seasons of the Church calendar is the early Church's celebration of Christ's death and resurrection. Saint Irenaeus, who lived during the second century A.D. claimed that the celebration of Christ's death and resurrection went back to the time of Saint Polycarp, a disciple of the Apostle John. This means that the Church, from the very earliest of times, had already begun to celebrate the life of Jesus.

Consequently, an entire liturgical year was created in order to walk the Church, both corporately and individually, through the life and ministry of Jesus. The Church's faith was not something upheld and taught only on Sundays, it was something each member of the Church lived every day. It was an experience.

Through the reading of Scripture, the celebration of the Eucharist, and the observance of the feast days and fast days, we celebrate the major events in the life of Christ and in the life of the church. We are constantly molded and shaped as we walk through these seasons. The Church's seasons don't just repeat, they reshape us and reform us, making us more and more like Jesus. In other words, the seasons of the Church are how we are shaped into God's people.

As we move through the seasons of the Church, we continuously marvel at what God has done for us through His holy son, Jesus Christ. He has made a way back to Him, back to abundant life. Because we are so filled with gratitude we want to serve and honor God not just on Sundays but every day with every part of our lives. The seasons of the Church were created so that our everyday lives would be permeated with the Spirit of the Living God. The seasons do not take precedence over interior formation but are a means of enrichment.

This book was written to help you move into a deeper, daily walk with God. By incorporating the seasons of the Church into our lives, we are able to more intentionally honor God with our lives and we are able to move not only individually, but also as a family, as a church and as the church universal through the life and mysteries of Christ.

May you be richly blessed as you embrace this marvelous gift - the seasons of the Church.

WHAT IS ADVENT?

*A*ll of Scripture is a sacred love story, the love of God the Father for His people. It is a story filled with expectation, longing and fulfillment. From the beginning, God has lovingly walked with us, called to us, searched for us even when we turned from Him over and over again. Throughout the Old Testament, God repeatedly calls his people back to himself and time and again we remain unfaithful. He sends the prophets to call His people back and with the call to return comes a promise, a promise of hope, a promise of redemption, a promise of restoration, a promise to be made again into the people we were meant to be, a people fully alive in God.

These saving acts of God will be accomplished through a Savior who will come to rescue us and bring us back into fellowship with God. No longer will we strive with God.

No longer will we be separated from Him. No longer will we turn from Him because through His Savior, His Messiah, His Anointed one, He will give us new hearts and set us free.

Each Advent, we wait with the prophets and with all of creation for the birth of the promised Savior. The prophets' call grows silent for 400 years and then suddenly, out of nowhere, the Almighty God stretches forth His hand to a small town and calls a seemingly insignificant young girl and she says "yes." The God of the universe humbles himself and makes himself flesh, to fully walk with us in our joy and sorrow. He takes the form of a helpless babe. It is a great mystery. It is the Incarnation. It is God with us, Emmanuel.

This event is so spectacular, so exceptional, and so important that time itself starts here. The first day of the Church year is the first Sunday of Advent. Advent comes from the Latin "Adventus" and simply means "coming." The season of Advent begins four Sundays before Christmas and is a time for us to prepare not only for the celebration of the coming of Christ as a babe on Christmas Day, but also for the second coming of Christ when he will return in triumph to judge the world.

In her book, *Around the Year with the Trapp Family*, Maria Von Trapp says that the "whole of Advent is characterized by the boundless desire for the coming of Christ expressed in the liturgy" of the Church. And so we cry out with the Church and with all our hearts: "Maranatha!

Come, Lord Jesus!" And, like creation from Adam until the last prophet, or like Mary expectant with child, we embrace the mystery of waiting and we lovingly prepare our hearts. Just like the season of Lent is a time to prepare for Easter, the season of Advent is the time to prepare our hearts for the coming of Christ. It is during this time that we look to John the Baptist, the last and greatest prophet sent by God to prepare us for the Messiah. We turn inward and pray for the Holy Spirit to examine our hearts and our motives and to reveal anything that is unclean within us. We repent of our sins and we strive to offer fruits worthy of repentance.

Advent is also a time to remember those less fortunate than us, those who, like the Holy Family, have very little in this life and no place to rest their weary heads. It is a time to collect alms for the poor and to stretch out our hands in a spirit of charity to bless and to heal those around us. The preparation of Advent is given so that our souls may be restored and so that we might be led, as a Church, into a "more profound delight in His birth" (Maria Von Trapp).

Although the Church celebrates the season, Advent is absent from the everyday world in which we live. And sadly, it is also often missing from our own homes. Our entire Christian faith is based upon the birth, death, and resurrection of Jesus. However, in the world in which we live, we are given no time to prepare for the birth of our Lord and Savior and then no time to celebrate it once we get there. Christmas decorations explode into stores right after the Halloween merchandise comes down and then the season abruptly ends the day after Christmas. The very heart of both Advent and Christmas - Jesus - has been ripped away and all we are left with is an abstract "Holiday" season. Songs of "Frosty the Snowman" and "Santa Claus Is Coming to Town" blare over the loudspeaker and we are wished a "Happy Holidays" rather than a "Merry Christmas" by the checkout clerk. The Christmas season has become completely devoid of Christ. For the wider world, it is no better than a hyper-commercialized pagan Holiday.

But, let us, as God's people, reclaim the beauty and longing of the season of Advent and celebrate it with the Church throughout the world. Hear these words from the Bidding Prayer which is said each year at the Advent Festival of Lessons and Carols:

"Beloved in Christ, in this season of Advent, let it be our care and delight to prepare ourselves to hear again the message of the Angels, and in heart and mind to go even unto Bethlehem, to see the Babe lying in a manger. Let us read and mark in Holy Scripture the tale of the loving purposes of God from the first days of our disobedience unto the glorious Redemption brought us by his holy Child; and let us look forward to the yearly remembrance of his birth with hymns and songs of praise." *Book of Occasional Services (2004), p. 31.*

HOW TO CELEBRATE ADVENT

*A*dvent properly observed is radically different from the way most of us celebrate the Christmas season. It is a time of waiting, longing and joy-filled expectation. It is a time to emphasize in every way delayed rather than instant gratification. Advent songs are sung rather than Christmas songs, sweets are limited to feast days until Christmas, the tree is not fully decorated until Christmas Eve, and the list goes on and on. All of these things are done intentionally in order to emphasize a spirit of preparation, waiting and longing for the fulfillment of God's promise. Although properly observing Advent can be difficult (especially when the wider world skips it altogether), the feeling of joy when Christmas Eve finally arrives will be that much greater.

This is what celebrating Advent does, it takes the chaos and the frantic rush of our lives and it forces us to slow down. We are given, as a family, time to prepare our hearts for the coming of Christ so that when Christmas finally arrives, we greet the day with true joy.

IDEAS FOR PERSONAL OR FAMILY COMMITMENTS DURING ADVENT

Personal or family commitments help us to set this time apart as holy. They help us to prepare our hearts.

Prepare Together.

Commit to preparing your home for Advent. Incorporate the five senses into your home. Put out a candle that reminds you of winter. Create an Advent playlist. Cook some of the Advent recipes found at the back of the book. Add seasonal decor to your home that reminds you of Advent. Use the liturgical color in your home. The use of colors to differentiate liturgical seasons became a common practice in the Western church in the fourth century. The colors were created to give a visual cue to everyone in attendance as to what season they were celebrating. The liturgical color for the season of Advent is purple or blue. The purple symbolizes Christ's royalty and our penitence and the blue symbolizes preparation. The liturgical color also changes for special days throughout the season and will be noted in the book.

Eat Together.

Decide on the number of times during the week that you will eat together and try to stick to this commitment.

Make sure that no devices are allowed at the table. When you eat together, pick something to eat that everyone will enjoy so there is no strife at the table. Take your time eating the meal and explain to your children that even though they might be done eating, they will remain at the table to share in the family time.

Fast Together.

Try to limit the amount of sweets that you eat to the special feast days. Introduce Advent songs sing them instead of Christmas carols. Wait until Christmas Eve to fully decorate your Christmas tree. Watch less television and spend more quality time as a family. Commit to a daily devotion personally or with your family.

Pray Together.

Find a time for devotions that best suits your family: at the breakfast table, around the table after dinner, in the children's bedroom right before bed, etc. Give your children roles to play in your time of devotion. Allow them to light the candles, snuff out the candles, read the scriptures, pray, pick the song that you sing, etc. This is a wonderful way to show your children that they are an important part of God's family and to help them feel included.

Serve Together.

Collect alms for the poor. Set up a prominent place for your alms container. Set an example by adding your own money to the container. Talk to them about why we give to the poor. Ask them to identify the poor in your community. Make a point to serve those in need as a family during Advent.

PUTTING IT ALL TOGETHER

Decide personally or as a family how you will mark this time. Make it official by writing your commitments down and hanging them in a prominent place in your home like the refrigerator or on the kitchen wall.

If you have children, allow your children to decorate your commitments with things reminding them of Advent like the Advent color, an Advent wreath, the Holy Family journeying to Bethlehem, sweets with a big "X" over them, or the particular family commitments you have made.

Talk to your children about the way the family will walk through Advent. Explain to them that how you walk through this time as a family will look very different from how the world behaves during this time of the year. Remind them that everything you do during Advent is done in order to prepare our hearts for Jesus. Talk to them about parents who are about to have a baby. They not only open their hearts to the child that is yet to be born but they also prepare the child's room, get clothing and blankets ready and pick out a name. We, as God's people, are the same way as those parents. We not only prepare for the birth of Jesus in our hearts, but in our actions as well. As God's people, we celebrate Advent to remind ourselves that we are sinners and that we get too caught up in our own wants and desires: what we will eat; what we will wear; what we want to play with, etc.

Make sure that your children understand that God will not be angry with them if they eat a cookie or sing a Christmas carol before Christmas Eve. Advent is something we do for ourselves to help us sanctify the time and remember who we are and what has been done for us by Jesus. It does not help God to love us more, nor will he love us any less. He already loves each of us more than we can imagine.

ADVENT TRADITIONS FOR THE ENTIRE SEASON

There are many traditional ways to observe Advent. All of the following things are given as aids to focus our attention and to mark the passage of Advent. Choose as many as you would like but don't overwhelm yourself or your family with too many. They are given to enrich our lives, not to burden us down. After choosing some, incorporate them into your daily and weekly devotions.

ADVENT CALENDAR

Created in Germany in the nineteenth-century, Advent calendars are used to mark the days of Advent. For each day of Advent, there is either a window that reveals something when opened or a pouch which might hold one or more of the following: a trinket, a piece of candy, a coin, a picture or a Bible verse.

Have your children make their own Advent calendars at home. They can be made to look like a home, church or manger scene with many flaps. Behind each flap have them draw an Advent symbol such as a star, an angel, or another Christian symbol. On the twenty-third of December, all of the flaps should be open, but the big entrance flap is still closed. The biggest flap is opened on Christmas Eve and reveals the Holy Child in the manger. Under the Christmas Eve flap, the Advent calendar message traditionally reads: "Today you will know that the Lord is coming to save us and in the morning you will see his glory" (Exodus 16:6-7).

ADVENT MUSIC

Advent is the season for Advent songs. Advent songs are very different from the songs of Christmas. Think about "O Come, O Come Emmanuel" and the deep desire for redemption conveyed in the words. The songs of Advent are filled with great longing and expectation. To sing Advent songs rather than Christmas carols will be difficult for most people and contrary to what is being played in secular spaces, but focusing on the songs of Advent will only heighten and further emphasize Advent's themes. Not singing Christmas carols throughout Advent will only make them that much more powerful when we finally sing them on Christmas Eve. To make the most of what Advent has to offer musically, attend an Advent Lessons and Carols Service and listen to a good production of Handel's Messiah.

ADVENT WREATH

The Advent Wreath is a wreath of evergreens with equidistant candles and a central candle. The wreath is a wonderful visual symbol marking our passage of time through Advent. The Advent Wreath provides a visual focus for your evening family devotions.

The wreath is used as a sign to your family that Christians are joyfully waiting for the coming of our Savior, the Christ Child, as every Sunday in Advent a new candle is lighted. Make an Advent Wreath from a kit or on your own and hang it from the ceiling or place it in the center of your dining table. Gather your family every Sunday night for Evening Prayer, light the appropriate number of candles and pray through your family devotions.

The Advent wreath is full of beautiful symbols. The shape of the circle represents eternity. Evergreens are a traditional Christmas decoration that represent the eternal nature of God. Candles represent a time of preparation and purification as well as the light or presence of Christ. The color of the candles is also symbolic. Violet represents penitence as we prepare our hearts for the birth of our Savior. Blue is also used instead of violet to symbolize a sense of expectancy. The rose or pink candle represents Mary, the willing servant of God and the mother of our Lord. The white candle represents Christ and is lit on Christmas Eve.

The order each candle is lit is also symbolic.

The first candle is the Patriarch's Candle and reminds us of the great patriarchs of the Bible who faithfully followed God and who prepared for the coming of the Messiah. On this day, a violet or blue candle is lit.

The second candle is the Prophet's Candle and reminds us of the great prophets of the Bible who faithfully followed God and called God's people to return to God and to faithfulness. On this day, a violet or blue candle is lit along with the Patriarch's candle.

The third candle is the Virgin Mary Candle and reminds us of the faithfulness of Mary who responded to God's call to bear the Christ. A rose or pink candle is lit along with the Patriarch's candle and Prophet's candle.

Note: The third Sunday of Advent is often called Gaudete Sunday. Gaudete means rejoice! The opening antiphon for this day is "Rejoice in the Lord always" which in Latin is Gaudete in Domino Semper. On this day the penitent mood lifts and we move into a more joyful time of expectancy as the celebration of Christ's birth draws closer.

The fourth candle is the John the Baptist Candle. Jesus calls John the greatest of all prophets. He came to proclaim the coming of the Messiah and to prepare the way of the Lord. On this day, a violet or blue candle is lit along with the Patriarch's candle, the Prophet's Candle and the Virgin Mary Candle.

The fifth and central candle is the Christ Candle and represents the birth of our Savior. Along with the other four candles, the Christ Candle is lit on Christmas Eve, Christmas Day and the subsequent twelve Days of Christmas.

CAROLING

Nativity or Christmas Carols were folk songs written and sung by the local community. Saint Francis of Assisi is credited with making Christmas carols an important part of church services by introducing them during a Christmas Midnight Mass in 1223.

Caroling in the streets and the town square soon became a favorite way to celebrate the joy of Christ's birth. Caroling is one of the oldest customs in Great Britain and goes back to the Middle Ages when beggars, seeking food, money, or drink, would wander the streets singing holiday songs. The traditional period to sing carols is from Saint Thomas's Day (December 21) until Christmas morning.

CHRISTKINDL OR THE CHRIST CHILD TRADITION

In many European countries, there is the tradition of the Christkindl. On the first Sunday of Advent, right after evening devotions, the mother of the family appears with a bowl filled with the names of the family members on slips of paper. The bowl is passed around and everyone takes a slip of paper with a name on it. The person whose name one has drawn is now in one's special care throughout Advent. From this day until Christmas, one has to do as many little favors for him or her as one can. One has to provide at least one surprise every single day - but without ever being found out. Maria Von Trapp tells us that this special relationship is called "Christkindl in the old country, where children believe that the Christmas tree and the gifts are brought down by the Christ child himself. The person whose name I have drawn and who is under my care becomes for me the little helpless Christ Child in the manger." This creates a wonderful atmosphere of joyful suspense, kindness and thoughtfulness. What a special way to observe Advent as a Family!

THE CHRISTMAS CRIB

The manger that held baby Jesus is extremely symbolic for Christians. It holds a Eucharistic message: the manger that once held grain for the animals, now holds the very Bread of Life. It is a powerful anticipation of the mystery of Holy Communion. In many countries, a large wooden crib or manger is placed in the living room on the first Sunday of Advent. The crib is empty and next to it is placed a bag of straw. Every evening, after family prayers, the children in the family come to the crib and place one piece of straw in the crib for every sacrifice or good deed done that day. All of these good deeds and sacrifices are done in order to please the Christ Child. This is an amazing opportunity to encourage your children to prepare for the coming of Christ. You might even make it a tradition to build the manger as a family each year in the days before Advent and then fill it with straw throughout the season.

THE CHRISTMAS TREE

Saint Boniface, an English missionary to Germany in the eighth century, is credited with the creation of the first authentic Christmas tree. He was responsible for firmly establishing the Church in German speaking countries.

When Saint Boniface arrived in Germany, many of the pagan tribes worshiped the trees. In order to show the tribes that the trees themselves had no power, he cut down a tree. He then brought the tree indoors, decorated it with lights and taught the people that they should worship the true God who created the trees. He died a martyr's death and is now widely revered in Germany.

Traditionally, the Christmas Tree was not fully decorated until Christmas Eve and was decorated by the parents in secret. When the decorated Christmas tree was revealed to the children, it was with the understanding that the Christ Child decorated the tree.

Note: If you already have have a tradition of decorating the tree before Christmas Eve, that's ok! You could also compromise by putting the tree up on the first day of Advent and decorate it only with Jesse Tree ornaments and then fully deck the tree on Christmas Eve. Then, after prayerfully moving through Advent, decorating the Christmas tree on Christmas Eve will bring the anticipation of Jesus' birth to a delightful height.

CHRISTMAS BAKING

Advent is a wonderful time to bake with children. Baking helps to further emphasize the themes of Advent: preparing gifts for others and waiting until Christmas to enjoy our gifts. Traditionally, most of the Christmas baking was done on Saint Thomas Day (December 21). If any baking was done before then, none of it was eaten (or even tasted!) in order to further emphasize the themes of waiting and anticipation in Advent. What a wonderful way to emphasize the joy of the great feast we will celebrate fully on Christmas Day.

CHRISTMAS GIFTS

In most countries around the world, Christmas gifts are given on Christmas Eve, Christmas Day or the Twelve

Days of Christmas. However, in some eastern countries, gift giving is reserved for Epiphany in order to celebrate the bringing of gifts by the Magi to the Christ Child.

A major difference between the way the majority of the Christian world and the United States gives gifts has to do with who is believed to give the gifts. In the United States, the historical figure of Saint Nicholas, whose feast day is celebrated on December 6, has largely been replaced by the fictitious character known as Santa Claus. Children are told that Santa Claus is responsible for all (or most) of the gifts on Christmas Day. However, in the rest of the Christian world, children are taught that it is the Christ Child who decorates their Christmas tree and who gives them all of their gifts.

Attributing all gifts to the Christ Child is a wonderful way to demonstrate to your children that "every good and perfect gift" comes from God and that the greatest of these gifts is Jesus, sent to save us from our sins and bring us back to God.

Make sure that you teach your children as they grow up that the focus of gift giving should be on what we give rather than on what we receive. We give because God first freely gave to us. He held nothing back! He even gave us his most precious gift - his only Son. A great way to emphasis the act of giving could be to encourage your children to make their gifts by hand. If every gift given by your children had been lovingly and thoughtfully handmade, how much more meaningful would they be?

Traditionally, Christmas gifts were given to the poor. Because Jesus humbled himself and became poor, the poor were the ones who were honored with gifts. Since Jesus said that everything we do for the poor, we do for him, have your family focus on collecting alms and buying them gifts.

CHRISMONS

Chrismons are a more recent tradition. They were created by a woman named Frances Spencer for her church. They gained popularity among churches across the United States. Chrismons mean "Christ monograms" and are traditionally white and gold designs made from Christian symbols that signify Christ. They are often hung on a Christmas tree in the church. The symbols include stars, crosses, fish, crowns, and the alpha and omega. The symbols remind us of Christ's identity and His story. They can be made from paper or metal but most of them are made from needlepoint.

THE GREAT ADVENT CANDLE

Traditionally, a lighted candle has always symbolized the presence of Christ. The Great Advent Candle is a tall white candle which is lit every night of Advent. Great Advent Candles are notched for every day of Advent and are sold in specialty stores. You can also buy a basic white pillar candle and if you like, you can make marks on the candle for each day of Advent. Burn the candle each night and let it burn to the next notch. Let the Great Advent Candle and the Advent wreath be the only light for your family's prayer time. Explain to your children that the candle is the symbol of Jesus, the Light of the World, and is a reminder of the world's spiritual darkness as we wait for the coming of Christ.

THE JESSE TREE

Jesse was the father of the great King David of the Old Testament. In Church art, a design developed showing the relationship of Jesus with Jesse and other biblical figures. This design showed a branched tree growing from a reclining figure of Jesse. The various branches had pictures of other Old and New Testament figures who were ancestors of Jesus. At the top of the tree were figures of Mary and Jesus. This design was often used in stained glass windows in the great medieval cathedrals of Europe.

The modern Jesse tree is an Advent custom using a collection of symbols depicting the biblical story of man's redemption from Adam and Eve to Jesus. The use of Jesse Tree ornaments helps us to better understand Jesus as fully human and fully divine and is a way to reclaim Christmas ornaments as sacred. The symbolic ornaments of the Jesse Tree vary from family to family and can be store bought or homemade. The ornaments are hung on a small tabletop sized tree or on a branch brought in from outside. They can also be used on your Christmas tree.

Add one ornament to the Jesse Tree each day, starting on December 1st.

Make your own Jesse Tree ornaments. Paint the symbols onto wooden rounds, carve wood into shapes, embroider them onto linen rounds which are then sewn onto round hoops to hold their shape, paint them on paper, or get your children to use their imagination and make their own!

Jesse Tree Scriptures and Ornament Ideas (These symbols are only suggestions)

- **December 1** *Creation*: Gen. 1:1-31; 2:1-4 *Symbols*: sun, moon, stars, animals, earth
- **December 2** *Adam and Eve*: Gen. 2:7-9, 18-24 *Symbols:* tree, man, woman
- **December 3** *Fall of Man*: Gen. 3:1-7 and 23-24 *Symbols:* tree, serpent, apple with bite
- **December 4** *Noah*: Gen. 6:5-8, 13-22; 7:17, 23, 24; 8:1, 6-22 *Symbols*: ark, animals, dove, rainbow
- **December 5** *Abraham*: Gen. 12:1-3 *Symbols:* torch, sword, mountain
- **December 6** *Isaac:* Gen. 22:1-14 *Symbols:* bundle of wood, altar, ram in bush
- **December 7** *Jacob*: Gen. 25:1-34; 28:10-15 *Symbols:* kettle, ladder
- **December 8** *Joseph:* Gen. 37:23-28; 45:3-15 *Symbols:* bucket, well, silver coins, tunic
- **December 9** *Moses:* Ex. 2:1-10 *Symbols:* baby in basket, river and rushes

- **December 10** *Samuel:* 1 Sam. 3:1-18 *Symbols:* lamp, temple
- **December 11** *Jesse:* 1 Sam. 16:1-13 *Symbols:* crimson robe, shepherd's staff
- **December 12** *David:* 1 Sam. 17:12-51 *Symbols:* slingshot, 6-pointed star
- **December 13** *Solomon:* 1 Kings 3:5-14, 16-28 *Symbols:* scales of justice, temple, two babies and sword
- **December 14** *Joseph*: Matt. 1:18-25 *Symbols*: hammer, saw, chisel, angle
- **December 15** *Mary*: Matt. 1:18-25; Luke 1:26-38 *Symbols*: lily, crown of stars, pierced heart
- **December 16** *John the Baptist:* Mark 1:1-8 *Symbols:* shell with water, river
- *Note - On December 17, the Church begins to intensify its preparations for Christmas with the use of the "O Antiphons" therefore the symbols from December 17 on will be based on the "O Antiphons".*
- **December 17** *Jesus is Wisdom:* I Corinthians 1:24 *Symbols:* oil lamp, open book
- **December 18** *Jesus is Lord:* Ex. 3:2; 20:1 *Symbols:* burning bush, stone tablets
- **December 19** *Jesus is Flower of Jesse*: Isaiah 11:1-3 *Symbols:* flower, plant with flower
- **December 20** *Jesus is Key of David*: Isaiah 22:22 *Symbols:* key, broken chains
- **December 21** *Jesus is the Radiant Dawn:* Psalm 19:6-7 *Symbols:* sun rising or high in sky

- **December 22** *Jesus is King of the Gentiles*: Psalm 2:7-8; Ephesians 2:14-20 *Symbols*: crown, scepter
- **December 23** *Jesus is Emmanuel*: Isaiah 7:14; 33:22 *Symbols*: tablets of stone, chalice and host
- **December 24** *Jesus is Light of the World*: John 1:1-14 *Symbols*: candle, flame, sun

NATIVITY SCENE OR CRÈCHE

From the very first century of Christianity, pilgrimages were made to the site where Jesus was born in Bethlehem. An altar was built where the manger had been and the Church of the Nativity was built over the site. Saint Francis of Assisi is credited with the idea of bringing the nativity scene into his hometown.

Saint Francis' nativity scene was created in Greccio, near Assisi on Christmas Eve, in 1223 and used real people and animals. The idea of a nativity scene in one's own town quickly spread throughout Christendom. Shortly thereafter, people began to construct large nativity scenes in their own homes. As the years have passed, the nativity scenes have gotten smaller and now fit on a table or shelf.

Traditionally, the nativity figures were set up in a certain way. Like an Advent Calendar, figures are slowly added to the scene. As Christmas Day approaches, Mary, Joseph and the donkey move closer to the manger where the other animals are waiting. The shepherds and sheep also move closer until they finally arrive on Christmas Eve when baby Jesus is also added to the manger. The Wise

Men are the farthest away and move closer and closer until they finally arrive on the Feast of the Epiphany on January 6.

STOCKINGS

The traditional story associated with stockings involves Saint Nicholas. Legend has it that there was a poor man who had three daughters. The man had no money to get his daughters married, and he was worried about what would happen to them after his death. Saint Nicholas was passing through town when he heard the villagers talking about the girls and he wanted to help. He knew that the old man would never accept charity so he decided to help in secret. He waited until it was night and crept into the house with a bag of gold coins for each girl. As he was looking for a place to put three bags, he noticed stockings hung over the mantelpiece for drying. He put one bag in each stocking and left. When the girls and their father woke up the next morning, they found the bags of gold coins and the girls were able to get married. This led to the custom of children hanging stockings or putting out shoes, eagerly awaiting gifts from Saint Nicholas on his feast day, December 6.

ADVENT TRADITIONS FOR SPECIFIC DAYS

*I*n addition to the overall season of Advent, there are special days to celebrate; feast days where we remember special people in the life of the church and the days of anticipation leading up to Christmas Day.

A special note about feast days in the church - they always start at sundown on the day before.

THE EVE OF SAINT NICHOLAS (DECEMBER 5)

Saint Nicholas was a real person. He was the Bishop of Myra in the 4th century and took part in the great church council of Nicaea which gave us the Nicene Creed - the one we recite every Sunday in Church! It is said that he was extremely concerned with the welfare of children and there are many legends about his good deeds.

The traditional story associated with Saint Nicholas involves stockings. Legend has it that there was a poor man who had three daughters. The man had no money to get his daughters married, and he was worried about what would happen to them after his death. Saint Nicholas was passing through town when he heard the villagers talking about the girls and he wanted to help. He knew that the old man would never accept charity so he decided to help in secret. He waited until it was night and crept into the house with a bag of gold coins for each girl. As he was looking for a place to put three bags, he noticed stockings hung over the mantelpiece for drying. He put one bag in each stocking and left. When the girls and their father woke up the next morning, they found the bags of gold coins and the girls were able to get married. This led to the custom of children hanging stockings or putting out shoes, eagerly awaiting gifts from Saint Nicholas on his feast day, December 6.

Most of the Christian world still remembers Saint Nicholas and celebrates his life on December 6. He is depicted as a bishop of the church with his cope, mitre, and crozier. When people dress up as Saint Nicholas, they dress like a bishop and when they make cookies on his feast day, the cookies are cut out in the shape of a bishop with a staff. But in the United States he has become known as Santa Claus or Jolly Old St. Nick. Instead of celebrating him on his feast day, we celebrate him all season long, especially on Christmas Day where he is believed to give gifts (with the help of elves and flying reindeer) on Christmas. Celebrating Saint Nicholas Day and the eve of his feast are an excellent way to re-educate our children on the true role of Saint Nicholas. He cared for children and for the poor. He gave to people who were in need. He would never have wanted to be the focus of Christmas! Saint Nicholas gave because Jesus had already given everything. Saint Nicholas would point us all back to Jesus.

Ways to Celebrate

Traditionally, the father of the family dresses as a bishop and visits the family, reminding the children that Christmas is drawing near and urging them to prepare their hearts for the coming of Christ. In South America, children write their letters of request to the Christ Child and it is the bishop, Saint Nicholas who picks them up and delivers them to Jesus.

Make Speculatius (see recipe in the recipe section), a traditional cookie made in the Rhineland. It is a crispy, buttery cookie, specially made for Saint Nicholas Day and it is made in the shape of a bishop with a staff.

Have your children put out their Christmas stockings on this night. Fill them while they are asleep with candies and cookies.

THE FEAST OF SAINT NICHOLAS (DECEMBER 6)

Ways to Celebrate

When the children discover their filled stockings on Saint Nicholas Day, tell them the story of Saint Nicholas and the three girls. Explain to them that our stockings are filled today to remind us of the way that Saint Nicholas blessed those in need. Today we are called to remember those in need too.

It is traditional in Germany to make Lebkuchen or German honey cakes on this day. A Dutch tradition is to make Bisschopswijn or Bishop's Wine which is a spiced wine. It is also traditional to make more Speculatius cookies on this day. Recipes for each of these items can be found at the end of this book.

SAINT LUCY'S DAY (DECEMBER 13TH)

Saint Lucy or Santa Lucia was a young girl who grew up in Italy in the 4th century. She is one of the earliest Christian martyrs. She was killed by the Romans in 304BC because of her religious beliefs. St. Lucy was born into a rich family but desired to dedicate her whole life to God and to give all of her worldly possessions to the poor. She brought food to persecuted Christians that were hiding in the Roman catacombs. The catacombs were dark and in order to find your way around, you needed to carry candles. St. Lucy wanted to bring as much food as possible to the people but needed to keep both of her hands free. She solved this problem by attaching candles to a wreath on her head.

St. Lucy's Day is celebrated in many countries such as Norway, Denmark, Italy, Croatia, Bosnia, Bavaria, Hungary, Sweden, Scandinavia, Iceland and Austria. Every aspect of the day has special significance since it comes on one of the darkest days of winter. The name Lucy or Lucia means "light" and she is remembered wearing a crown of candles all of which bring light and hope to the darkest time of winter. St. Lucy is also depicted wearing a white dress which symbolizes her baptismal robe and a red sash which symbolizes her martyrdom.

Ways to Celebrate

Make Cuccia with your family (see recipe in the recipe section of the book). In Italy, Sicilians have a legend that a great famine ended on St. Lucy's feast day when ships loaded with grain entered the harbor. So, on St. Lucy's day, it is traditional to eat whole grains instead of bread. The dish that they typically eat is called cuccia which is boiled wheat berries mixed with ricotta and honey.

In Croatia and Hungary, it is traditional to plant grains of wheat on Saint Lucy's Day. Since agriculture was the mainstay of the people, wheat was extremely important to the community and was a symbol of sustenance and prosperity. Wheat also symbolized Jesus as the bread of life. Every year on St. Lucy's Day wheat seeds are planted in soil on a pretty dish with a candle placed in the middle. If the seeds are kept moist, they will germinate and grow into plants that will be several inches high by Christmas. The new green shoots remind us of the new life born in Bethlehem. The candle reminds us of the Light of Christ that St. Lucy shared with her life.

Plant Christmas wheat with your family. To plant wheat seeds, fill a pot 5 to 6 inches deep with dirt. Sprinkle the wheat seeds across the soil and press in so that they are just barely covered by dirt. Place a candle in the center of the dirt. Keep in a moderately warm room and water daily. The plants will reach their full growth by Christmas Day and they will live until the beginning of January. As the plants begin to grow, place a pretty Christmas ribbon around them and tie with a bow.

In Sweden, Denmark, Norway, and Finland, they celebrate St. Lucy's day with large processions. A girl is chosen to be St. Lucy. She wears a white gown with a red sash and a crown of candles on her head. She leads a procession of women who are all holding candles. The candles symbolize bringing the Light of Christ into the world's darkness. Boys also participate in the procession, dressing as men associated with Christmastide, such as St. Stephen. The people sing the famous song, "Santa Lucia" while walking in the procession. The melody of the song comes from the traditional Neapolitan song, "Santa Lucia" but the lyrics are in the various Scandinavian languages of the country in which it is celebrated. The song describes the light with which Lucia overcomes the darkness.

On St. Lucy's Day there is also a more intimate celebration in the home. A daughter in the family is chosen to represent St. Lucy. She rises early in the morning wearing a white gown and a red sash. She wears a crown made from Lingonberry branches with 7 or 9 burning candles. The daughter wakes each family member up and serves them a cake called St. Lucy's Crown, saffron buns, or St. Lucy's Gingersnaps and fresh coffee. In Sweden and Scandinavia, they serve saffron buns and coffee with aquavit liquor. It is also traditional for the family to celebrate St. Lucy's Day at tea time or for cakes and pastries to be taken to the elderly.

Have your children create their own St. Lucy's Day celebration. Dress them in white with red sashes (anything white or red will do), make a crown of evergreens from your yard and make candles with construction paper and place them in the crown. Help your children to make coffee, cakes and buns (the recipes for each of these items can be found in the recipe section of the book) and then help them to serve the treats to the rest of the family. Your family could also take the treats and celebrate the day with the elderly. Another fun thing your family could do is look up the song "Santa Lucia" and play it while making the treats or while eating them.

THE LAST DAYS BEFORE CHRISTMAS

All of the great feasts of the Church year (Christmas, Epiphany, Easter and Pentecost) are followed by times of great merrymaking. It is not enough to celebrate only on the feast day itself, many days of feasting and merrymaking are given to fully celebrate the magnitude of the day. Christmas, however, is the only feast day that is also preceded by a time of merrymaking known in some countries as an octave (eight days) or a novena (nine days). The time before Christmas serves to increase our already growing sense of eagerness and expectation for the Christ to come.

SEEKING SHELTER, LA POSADA, GOLDEN NIGHTS (DECEMBER 16–24)

We are now moving into the last days before the birth of Christ, only nine days away, and so a remarkable build-up of traditions begins. December 16 is the night when an ancient custom is celebrated all over the world which is known by many different names; La Posada (The Inn) in Spanish-speaking countries, Golden Nights in Central Europe, and Seeking Shelter in Austria. The events in the journey of Mary and Joseph from Nazareth to Bethlehem are commemorated at this time.

Nine families from a local parish are chosen to participate in this event. Each family that participates acts as the innkeepers. Neighborhood children and adults act as the pilgrims who request lodging by going from house to house singing a traditional song requesting shelter for poor Mary and Joseph. The pilgrims carry small lit candles in their hands, and people carry small statues of

Joseph leading a donkey, on which Mary is riding. At each house, the "innkeepers" respond to the song by refusing lodging (also in song). Finally, on Christmas Eve, the weary travelers reach the final home, where Mary and Joseph are finally recognized and allowed to enter. In this last home where Mary and Joseph are finally received, candles are lit and everything is lovingly prepared.

The procession enters the home and everyone kneels around the Nativity scene to pray. A large cradle is waiting and a statue of the infant Jesus is placed on a bed of straw and gently rocked while everyone sings a traditional lullaby. In Latin American countries most people sing the beautiful "A La Rurru Niño" or "Babe in Arms." At the end of the long journey, everyone joins together for Christmas carols, feasting, firecrackers, and noisemakers.

In South America, children begin to write letters to the Christ child, telling him of their hopes for Christmas. Saint Nicholas picks the letters up and delivers them to baby Jesus. The letters are written from December 16-24 and are left next to the manger in the family's Nativity Scene.

Ways to Celebrate

Before your evening devotion, assemble the family and sing advent songs as you process the creche figures of Mary, Joseph and the don- key into the living room. Put the figures in a special place of honor and light a candle next to them. Remind your children that we are trying to create an atmosphere of consideration and unselfishness for Mary and Joseph.

A variation of this is to allow each of your children to make up for the harsh treatment that the holy couple received by hosting the figures in their room for the day. Instead of processing the figures into the living room, process them to the door of the first child's room while singing Advent songs. Explain to your children that when it is their turn, they should do everything possible to create a warm and loving atmosphere for Mary and Joseph. Suggest cleaning their room, clearing a spot on their dresser for the figures, placing fresh evergreens around the figures, or ribbons, etc.

Have your children write letters to baby Jesus, expressing their wishes for Christmas. This is a great way to re-educate your children, helping them to see that their Christmas gifts are from God, the giver of all good gifts.

O ANTIPHONS (DECEMBER 17–23)

The "O Antiphons" are another tradition which begins the final countdown to Christmas Day. The "O Antiphons" are brief scripturally based prayers focusing on the titles given to Christ by the prophet Isaiah. The Antiphons are traditionally prayed before and after "Mary's Song, the Magnificat", during Evening Prayer. One antiphon is prayed each evening, from December 17 until December 23. The Octave is completed by repeating all of the Antiphons on December 24.

Christians around the world are so eager for the birth of Christ, that we cry out with one voice for Christ to come - and come quickly! During these last days, our prayers and our expectations arise with an ever increasing crescendo. "O Come, O Come Emmanuel" is one of the Church's oldest and best loved hymns and is based on the "O Antiphons." Each stanza begins with one of the names for Jesus found in the Antiphons. It was meant to be sung during this octave with a new verse added each day.

Ways to Celebrate

Add the "O Antiphons" to your daily devotion. Sing "O Come, O Come Emmanuel" during your evening devotion. Show your children how each Antiphon is used in the song. Listen to the "O Antiphons" in Gregorian chant. (You can Google them and easily find them on Youtube!). Write the "O Antiphons" out as a family and read them as part of your evening devotion.

Here are the "O Antiphons":

December 17 - O Sapientia
O Wisdom, coming forth from the mouth
of the Most High,
reaching from one end to the other mightily,
and sweetly ordering all things:
Come and teach us the way of prudence.

December 18 – O Adonai
O Adonai, and leader of the House of Israel,
who appeared to Moses in the fire of the burning bush
and gave him the law on Sinai:
Come and redeem us with an outstretched arm.

December 19 - O Radix Jesse
O Root of Jesse, standing as a sign among the peoples;
before you kings will shut their mouths,
to you the nations will make their prayer:
Come and deliver us, and delay no longer.

December 20 - O Clavis David
O Key of David and scepter of the House of Israel;
you open and no one can shut;
you shut and no one can open:
Come and lead the prisoners from the prison house,
those who dwell in darkness and the shadow of death.

December 21 - O Oriens
O Morning Star,
splendor of light eternal and sun of righteousness:
Come and enlighten those who dwell in darkness
and the shadow of death.

December 22 - O Rex Gentium
O King of the nations, and their desire,
the cornerstone making both one:
Come and save the human race,
which you fashioned from clay.

December 23 - O Emmanuel
O Emmanuel, our King and our lawgiver,
the hope of the nations and their Savior:
Come and save us, O Lord our God.

FEAST OF SAINT THOMAS (DECEMBER 21)

Saint Thomas was one of Jesus' twelve apostles and is best
known for doubting that Jesus had been raised from the
dead when the other apostles told him they had seen Jesus
alive. He is thought to be the only Apostle who went
outside the Roman Empire to preach the Gospel. He is
also believed to have crossed the largest area, including
the Persian Empire and India. He was martyred for
leading an Indian Queen to faith in Jesus.

Ways to Celebrate

The Feast of Saint Thomas is the traditional day to begin
all of your Christmas baking. From now on, the house will
be filled with delicious smells as you bake for Christmas.
Include your children in as much of the baking as
possible. Remember that the baking that you do further
emphasizes the Advent themes of preparation and of
waiting. During this time, cook your choicest delicacies
and favorite treats. In many countries, particular cookies
are made only for Christmas. The cookies keep for a long
time and are often hung on the Christmas tree. What a
wonderful way to emphasize the significance of the
season with what we cook!

Throughout Austria, this is the day in which Kletzenbrot is baked. Kletzenbrot is a delicious bread with dried fruit in it. One large loaf is made for the family to eat on Christmas morning and then small loaves are made for every member of the family. In Germany, they make a bread called Cristollen which is folded up to look like Christ's diapers. (See recipes in the recipe section below)

Christmas cookies are also traditional during this time. Each country has its own particular kind; the United States and Great Britain make sugar cookies, Germany makes a sugar cookie called Springerles and a cookie called Lebkuchen which means Bread of Life. During this time, gingerbread cookies and gingerbread houses are also traditional.

Christians throughout the world use December 21-23 to prepare for the Christmas feast. During those days of preparation, every plate is piled high with cookies and treats. Although there are sweets all around, try to abstain from these sweets until Christmas Eve, knowing that this self denial will serve to increase the sense of anticipation and excitement leading up to Christmas.

With all of the baking and preparation, the children begin to see that the birth of Jesus is almost here! They will hardly be able to wait! This is an excellent opportunity to teach your children delayed gratification and to increase their desire for Christmas to arrive. And remember, the cookies and treats will taste that much better because everyone waited for them. By midnight on December 23, all baking should be completed and everything should be stored away.

CHRISTMAS EVE (DECEMBER 24)

The liturgical color is white or gold which symbolizes a high, holy day.

On Christmas Eve, we are suspended between two worlds - the world of darkness, sin and death and the new world of light promised through God's Messiah. On this day, the season of Advent draws to an end and the waiting and intentional preparation comes to a close. Christmas Eve is our last opportunity to heed the words of Saint John the Baptist to "prepare the way of the Lord." That is why, traditionally, Christmas Eve is a day for confession. Although we seek on this day to continue to prepare our hearts through confession and introspection, it is hard to contain our excitement because we know what happens at the stroke of midnight - the dawn of a new age comes with the birth of a Savior who will ransom us from sin and death and bring us back to God!

Ways to Celebrate

Traditionally, on the morning of December 24, most of the preparations for Christmas Day were completed. All cookies and treats had been hidden away. The kitchen looked sober and bare compared to the night before with nothing left out but the makings of a very frugal breakfast and lunch. This is so counter to have we celebrate now but Christmas Eve was one of the strictest fast days of the Christian year. All over the world, many people consumed no more than a cup of coffee and a piece of bread for breakfast and lunch was usually water and a small meatless meal. With these frugal meals, the holy season of Advent drew to a close.

It is also important to remember that Christmas Day is one of the highest feast days of the Christian year. We celebrate the birth of our Savior, Jesus. Christmas is what all of Advent has been getting us ready for. Christmas Eve should be a day of great anticipation and preparation. It is a wonderful opportunity to provide a sense of wonder and joy for your family that is focused on the birth of the Christ Child. If you can, make this a very special family day where everyone is together so that you can all watch, wait and prepare together. Allow and encourage your children to participate in all of these activities in order to create a sense of excitement. Christmas Eve is the final day of preparation for the Christmas Feast. Use this day as a time to prepare not only your home, food and clothes, but also to prepare your hearts for the joy to come.

Clean house!

As a final act of preparation, it is an Irish and Eastern European tradition to clean your house, return all borrowed items, and fix everything in your house that needs to be repaired. Read the final Advent calendar message - "Today you will know that the Lord is coming to save us and in the morning you will see his Glory!"

Hang the final Jesse Tree ornament and/or decorate your Christmas Tree.

Traditionally, in most parts of the world, the Christmas Tree is not put up until Christmas Eve. And when it is put up, it is oftentimes decorated by the parents in secret. When the decorated Christmas tree is revealed to the children, it is with the understanding that the Christ Child has blessed them with both the gifts and the decorations.

When the children wake up on Christmas Eve morning, have the door to the living room closed or curtained off. This will be the room where the tree and presents are put. Having the room closed off creates a sense of mystery and excitement for the children. Tell your children that no one is allowed to go in that room all day because this is where the Christ Child will bless them with gifts and a fully decorated tree. Post a sign on the door that says, "Please, Keep Out."

In the afternoon, send your children to their rooms for a time of quiet. Lay out special books on each of their pillows. Use Advent and Christmas books collected and saved until this time so that they are special and entertaining. They can also be taken by a loved one or relative to play outside or visit relatives. While the children are occupied, go into the room and prepare it for Christmas Eve. This is a great time for the parents to quietly reflect on the birth of Christ, to relax and to enjoy what this day means. Turn on Handel's Messiah while you work. Bring in the Christmas tree and fully decorate it. Refresh the Advent wreath and place the presents under the tree. Decorate the dining table and set it for a Christmas feast. Set out all of the cookies and foods you have prepared in advance. Place the Christmas crib by the tree. Place a bell next to the Nativity scene.

Serve an early Christmas Eve meal.

The Christmas Eve meal is really the very last moment of Advent. It is one of the two or three most important meals of the Christian year and is lovingly referred to as the "Holy Meal." It is a time where Christian families reaffirm their bonds of love and solidarity. Like Christmas Eve itself, the Christmas Eve meal, while still preparing us, is full of a joyful expectancy and is very celebratory in its nature. To reflect this, the Christmas Eve meal is a type of fast within a feast and meat is traditionally abstained from.

Each country has its own beautiful food traditions for this night mostly centering around a fish dish and lavish desserts. Every detail of the meal is rich with meaning. For instance, in many countries, the meal begins when the first star appears in the sky reminding us of the star of Bethlehem. The meal is candlelit with a large white candle in the center of the table symbolizing Christ as the Light of the World. Next to the candle is a round loaf of bread symbolizing Christ as the Bread of Life. Also, there are either twelve courses or twelve desserts served to represent the twelve disciples.

In Slavic countries, the floor and dining table are strewn with straw in honor of the stable and a white tablecloth representing the swaddling clothes that the infant Jesus was wrapped in is placed over the dining table's straw. The father breaks thin wafers with religious motifs known as the bread of angels and distributes a piece to each member of the family. As the father distributes the wafer pieces, he kisses each member of his family and wishes them a blessed Christmas.

The Christmas Eve meal is a beautiful symbol of love and unity in Christ. An extra place is always set at the table in honor of those who are absent. Traditionally, all members of the household sit down and eat together, including servants.

Attend the Christmas Eve service at your church.

If attending the service is not possible, after the Christmas Eve meal, gather the family around the Advent wreath one last time to have an evening devotion.

THE FEAST OF THE NATIVITY (CHRISTMAS DAY; DECEMBER 25)

The liturgical color is white or gold which means a high, holy day.

> "Joy to the World! The Lord has come!
> Let earth Receive her King!"

The birth of our long awaited Savior has finally come! Christmas Day is a feast day of the highest order. It is the day of days which celebrates the mystery of the Incarnation. The God of the universe humbled himself, took on flesh and walked among us. Finally we are able to celebrate with Christians all over the world the long awaited birth of Christ!

As we celebrate, we remember with joy the message of the angels, "Glory to God in the highest, and on earth peace, good will towards men" (Luke 2:14). It is with these words that we see clearly the loving hand of God. God has sent to us a Savior, his very son, Jesus, to redeem us, to set us free, and to bring us back to himself. What a glorious day this is!

Ways to Celebrate Christmas Day

It is traditional to greet each other with a kiss and the words: "Christ is Born!" to which the one being greeted responds: "Glorify Him!"

Attend Christmas Day services at your church or have a family devotion.

Remember that the bulk of the cooking should have been done by today so that Church can be attended and the immensity of the day be relished and enjoyed.

Sing Christmas carols! This is the time to sing them to yourself and with your family. Go over the words - really think about what they say and what they mean in your life.

This is also a day to remember and include the lonely and those who have recently lost loved ones.

If you have a nativity scene, start moving the three kings (placed some distance away) closer to the manger. Time the movement of the kings to last until the Feast of the Epiphany on January 6.

The Christmas Day Meal

This is the day for the festive and extravagant Christmas feast. The Christmas feast is the time to serve your choicest delicacies in order to celebrate the birth of our Savior. Christmas Day is also the time to serve the Christmas plum pudding.

To serve the Christmas pudding, the lights are turned out and warmed brandy or rum is poured over the pudding and set ablaze.

The flaming pudding is brought to the dinner table to be served as soon as the flame burns out. The pudding is filled with all of the good things of this world to remind us of Christ who will bring with Him on His birthday all the good things of heaven. After the meal, the family gathers in the Christmas room for a family devotion and the singing of carols. During this time in the Christmas room, serve something warm to drink like the French version of hot chocolate or spiced cider.

Christmas Symbols

The Christmas season is full of many rich symbols. Green and red are the traditional colors which represent the blood of Christ and the eternal life bought for us through Christ. Holly, a traditional Christmas plant, represents the crown of thorns. The Poinsettia, with its star-like petals represents the Star of Bethlehem. Rosemary has always been associated with Christmas because tradition has it that it was the bush used by Mary to dry baby Jesus' clothes.

ADVENT DEVOTIONS

he first Sunday of Advent is always four Sundays before Christmas. Because of this, the date of the first Sunday of Advent changes each year. We have provided readings for each day of Advent but in some years there will be more readings than you need. You may wish to incorporate the additional readings as Christmas approaches so that you can experience all of the readings for Advent.

We have also provided special prayers for each Sunday of Advent. When you come to a Sunday in your daily devotions, find the corresponding prayer in the Sundays of Advent section and light the appropriate candle.

THE FIRST SUNDAY OF ADVENT

Start the devotion with the lights lowered or turned off.

Leader: Light and peace, in Jesus Christ our Lord.
People: **Thanks be to God.**
Leader: Let us pray.

Leader:

God and Father of Abraham and Sarah, and all the patriarchs and matriarchs of old, you are our Father, too. Your love is revealed to us in Jesus Christ, Son of God and Son of David. Help us in preparing to celebrate his birth to make our hearts ready for your Holy Spirit to make his home among us. We ask this through Jesus Christ, the light who is coming into the world. **Amen.**

If you are using the Great Advent Candle, light it at this time. If you are using an Advent Wreath, The Patriarch Candle (the first violet or blue candle) is lit at this time.

All together
O gracious light, pure brightness of the everliving
Father in heaven, O Jesus Christ, holy and blessed!
Now as we come to the setting of the sun, and our eyes
behold the vesper light, we sing your praises, O God:
Father, Son, and Holy Spirit.
You are worthy at all times to be praised by happy
voices, O Son of God, O Giver of Life,
and to be glorified through all the worlds.

A Reading From Holy Scripture

Read: Genesis 1:1-5

---

1 In the beginning, God created the heavens and the earth. 2 The earth was without form and void, and darkness was over the face of the deep. And the Spirit of God was hovering over the face of the waters. 3 And God said, "Let there be light," and there was light. 4 And God saw that the light was good. And God separated the light from the darkness. 5 God called the light Day, and the darkness he called Night. And there was evening and there was morning, the first day.

Use this time for other Advent observances: adding hay to the Christmas Crib, hanging a new Jesse Tree ornament, or adding figures to the Nativity Scene.

The Lord's Prayer

All together
Our Father, who art in heaven,
hallowed be thy Name,
thy kingdom come, thy will be done,
on earth as it is in heaven.
Give us this day our daily bread.
And forgive us our trespasses,

as we forgive those who trespass against us.
And lead us not into temptation,
but deliver us from evil.
For thine is the kingdom,
and the power, and the glory,
for ever and ever. Amen.

The Blessing

Parents lay hands on each of your children and pray this blessing over them:

The Lord bless you and keep you. **Amen.**
The Lord make his face to shine upon you and be gracious to you. **Amen.**
The Lord lift up his countenance upon you and give you peace. **Amen.**

People: **Thanks be to God.**

The Advent devotions continue on the following pages. For your next devotion, turn to the devotion that corresponds to the date. For example, if the date is December 1st, turn to December 1st and continue your devotions through the rest of Advent.

NOVEMBER 28

Start the devotion with the lights lowered or turned off.

Leader: Light and peace, in Jesus Christ our Lord.
People: **Thanks be to God.**
Leader: Let us pray.

If you are using the Great Advent Candle, light it at this time. If you are using an Advent Wreath, light the appropriate candles.

All together
**O gracious light, pure brightness of the everliving
Father in heaven, O Jesus Christ, holy and blessed!
Now as we come to the setting of the sun, and our eyes
behold the vesper light, we sing your praises, O God:
Father, Son, and Holy Spirit.
You are worthy at all times to be praised by happy
voices, O Son of God, O Giver of Life,
and to be glorified through all the worlds.**

A Reading From Holy Scripture

Read: Genesis 1:6-13

---

6 And God said, "Let there be an expanse in the midst of the waters, and let it separate the waters from the waters." 7 And God made the expanse and separated the waters that were under the expanse

from the waters that were above the expanse. And it was so. **8** And God called the expanse Heaven. And there was evening and there was morning, the second day. **9** And God said, "Let the waters under the heavens be gathered together into one place, and let the dry land appear." And it was so. **10** God called the dry land Earth, and the waters that were gathered together he called Seas. And God saw that it was good. **11** And God said, "Let the earth sprout vegetation, plants yielding seed, and fruit trees bearing fruit in which is their seed, each according to its kind, on the earth." And it was so. **12** The earth brought forth vegetation, plants yielding seed according to their own kinds, and trees bearing fruit in which is their seed, each according to its kind. And God saw that it was good. **13** And there was evening and there was morning, the third day.

Use this time for other Advent observances: adding hay to the Christmas Crib, hanging a new Jesse Tree ornament, or adding figures to the Nativity Scene.

The Lord's Prayer

All together
**Our Father, who art in heaven,
hallowed be thy Name,
thy kingdom come, thy will be done,
on earth as it is in heaven.
Give us this day our daily bread.
And forgive us our trespasses,
as we forgive those who trespass against us.
And lead us not into temptation,
but deliver us from evil.
For thine is the kingdom,
and the power, and the glory,
for ever and ever. Amen.**

The Blessing

Parents lay hands on each of your children and pray this blessing over them:

The Lord bless you and keep you. **Amen.**
The Lord make his face to shine upon you and be gracious to you. **Amen.**
The Lord lift up his countenance upon you and give you peace. **Amen.**

People: **Thanks be to God.**

NOVEMBER 29

Start the devotion with the lights lowered or turned off.

Leader: Light and peace, in Jesus Christ our Lord.
People: **Thanks be to God.**
Leader: Let us pray.

If you are using the Great Advent Candle, light it at this time. If you are using an Advent Wreath, light the appropriate candles.

All together
**O gracious light, pure brightness of the everliving
Father in heaven, O Jesus Christ, holy and blessed!
Now as we come to the setting of the sun, and our eyes
behold the vesper light, we sing your praises, O God:
Father, Son, and Holy Spirit.
You are worthy at all times to be praised by happy
voices, O Son of God, O Giver of Life,
and to be glorified through all the worlds.**

A Reading From Holy Scripture

Read: Genesis 1:14-23

---

14 And God said, "Let there be lights in the expanse
of the heavens to separate the day from the night.
And let them be for signs and for seasons, and for
days and years, **15** and let them be lights in the

expanse of the heavens to give light upon the earth." And it was so. 16 And God made the two great lights —the greater light to rule the day and the lesser light to rule the night—and the stars. 17 And God set them in the expanse of the heavens to give light on the earth, 18 to rule over the day and over the night, and to separate the light from the darkness. And God saw that it was good. 19 And there was evening and there was morning, the fourth day. 20 And God said, "Let the waters swarm with swarms of living creatures, and let birds fly above the earth across the expanse of the heavens." 21 So God created the great sea creatures and every living creature that moves, with which the waters swarm, according to their kinds, and every winged bird according to its kind. And God saw that it was good. 22 And God blessed them, saying, "Be fruitful and multiply and fill the waters in the seas, and let birds multiply on the earth." 23 And there was evening and there was morning, the fifth day.

Use this time for other Advent observances: adding hay to the Christmas Crib, hanging a new Jesse Tree ornament, or adding figures to the Nativity Scene.

The Lord's Prayer

All together
Our Father, who art in heaven,
hallowed be thy Name,
thy kingdom come, thy will be done,
on earth as it is in heaven.
Give us this day our daily bread.
And forgive us our trespasses,
as we forgive those who trespass against us.
And lead us not into temptation,
but deliver us from evil.
For thine is the kingdom,
and the power, and the glory,
for ever and ever. Amen.

The Blessing

Parents lay hands on each of your children and pray this blessing over them:

The Lord bless you and keep you. **Amen.**
The Lord make his face to shine upon you and be gracious to you. **Amen.**
The Lord lift up his countenance upon you and give you peace. **Amen.**

People: **Thanks be to God.**

November 30

Start the devotion with the lights lowered or turned off.

Leader: Light and peace, in Jesus Christ our Lord.
People: **Thanks be to God.**
Leader: Let us pray.

If you are using the Great Advent Candle, light it at this time. If you are using an Advent Wreath, light the appropriate candles.

All together
O gracious light, pure brightness of the everliving
Father in heaven, O Jesus Christ, holy and blessed!
Now as we come to the setting of the sun, and our eyes
behold the vesper light, we sing your praises, O God:
Father, Son, and Holy Spirit.
You are worthy at all times to be praised by happy
voices, O Son of God, O Giver of Life,
and to be glorified through all the worlds.

A Reading From Holy Scripture

Read: Genesis 1:24-30

---

24 And God said, "Let the earth bring forth living creatures according to their kinds—livestock and creeping things and beasts of the earth according to their kinds." And it was so. **25** And God made the beasts of the earth according to their kinds and the livestock according to their kinds, and everything that creeps on the ground according to its kind. And God saw that it was good. **26** Then God said, "Let us make man in our image, after our likeness. And let them have dominion over the fish of the sea and over the birds of the heavens and over the livestock and over all the earth and over every creeping thing that creeps on the earth." **27** So God created man in his own image, in the image of God he created him; male and female he created them. **28** And God blessed them. And God said to them, "Be fruitful and multiply and fill the earth and subdue it, and have dominion over the fish of the sea and over the birds of the heavens and over every living thing that moves on the earth." **29** And God said, "Behold, I have given you every plant yielding seed that is on the face of all the earth, and every tree with seed in its fruit. You shall have them for food. **30** And to every beast of the earth and to every bird of the heavens and to everything that creeps on the earth, everything that has the breath of life, I have given every green plant for food." And it was so.

Use this time for other Advent observances: adding hay to the Christmas Crib, hanging a new Jesse Tree ornament, or adding figures to the Nativity Scene.

The Lord's Prayer

All together
Our Father, who art in heaven,
hallowed be thy Name,
thy kingdom come, thy will be done,
on earth as it is in heaven.
Give us this day our daily bread.
And forgive us our trespasses,
as we forgive those who trespass against us.
And lead us not into temptation,
but deliver us from evil.
For thine is the kingdom,
and the power, and the glory,
for ever and ever. Amen.

The Blessing

Parents lay hands on each of your children and pray this blessing over them:

The Lord bless you and keep you. **Amen.**
The Lord make his face to shine upon you and be gracious to you. **Amen.**
The Lord lift up his countenance upon you and give you peace. **Amen.**

People: **Thanks be to God.**

DECEMBER 1

Start the devotion with the lights lowered or turned off.

Leader: Light and peace, in Jesus Christ our Lord.
People: **Thanks be to God.**
Leader: Let us pray.

If you are using the Great Advent Candle, light it at this time. If you are using an Advent Wreath, light the appropriate candles.

All together
O gracious light, pure brightness of the everliving Father in heaven, O Jesus Christ, holy and blessed! Now as we come to the setting of the sun, and our eyes behold the vesper light, we sing your praises, O God: Father, Son, and Holy Spirit. You are worthy at all times to be praised by happy voices, O Son of God, O Giver of Life, and to be glorified through all the worlds.

A Reading From Holy Scripture

Read: Genesis 1:31-2:3

---

31 And God saw everything that he had made, and behold, it was very good. **1** And there was evening and there was morning, the sixth day. **2** Thus the heavens and the earth were finished, and all the host of them. **2** And on the seventh day God finished his work that he had done, and he rested on the seventh day from all his work that he had done. **3** So God blessed the seventh day and made it holy, because on it God rested from all his work that he had done in creation.

Use this time for other Advent observances: adding hay to the Christmas Crib, hanging a new Jesse Tree ornament, or adding figures to the Nativity Scene.

The Lord's Prayer

All together
Our Father, who art in heaven,
hallowed be thy Name,
thy kingdom come, thy will be done,
on earth as it is in heaven.
Give us this day our daily bread.
And forgive us our trespasses,
as we forgive those who trespass against us.
And lead us not into temptation,
but deliver us from evil.
For thine is the kingdom,
and the power, and the glory,
for ever and ever. Amen.

The Blessing

Parents lay hands on each of your children and pray this blessing over them:

The Lord bless you and keep you. **Amen.**
The Lord make his face to shine upon you and be gracious to you. **Amen.**
The Lord lift up his countenance upon you and give you peace. **Amen.**

People: **Thanks be to God.**

DECEMBER 2

Start the devotion with the lights lowered or turned off.

Leader: Light and peace, in Jesus Christ our Lord.
People: **Thanks be to God.**
Leader: Let us pray.

If you are using the Great Advent Candle, light it at this time. If you are using an Advent Wreath, light the appropriate candles.

All together
O gracious light, pure brightness of the everliving Father in heaven, O Jesus Christ, holy and blessed! Now as we come to the setting of the sun, and our eyes behold the vesper light, we sing your praises, O God: Father, Son, and Holy Spirit.
You are worthy at all times to be praised by happy voices, O Son of God, O Giver of Life, and to be glorified through all the worlds.

A Reading From Holy Scripture

Read: Genesis 2:4-17

---

4 These are the generations of the heavens and the earth when they were created, in the day that the Lord God made the earth and the heavens. 5 When no bush of the field was yet in the land and no small

plant of the field had yet sprung up—for the Lord God had not caused it to rain on the land, and there was no man to work the ground, **6** and a mist was going up from the land and was watering the whole face of the ground— 7 then the Lord God formed the man of dust from the ground and breathed into his nostrils the breath of life, and the man became a living creature.

8 And the Lord God planted a garden in Eden, in the east, and there he put the man whom he had formed. **9** And out of the ground the Lord God made to spring up every tree that is pleasant to the sight and good for food. The tree of life was in the midst of the garden, and the tree of the knowledge of good and evil. **10** A river flowed out of Eden to water the garden, and there it divided and became four rivers. **11** The name of the first is the Pishon. It is the one that flowed around the whole land of Havilah, where there is gold. **12** And the gold of that land is good; bdellium and onyx stone are there. **13** The name of the second river is the Gihon. It is the one that flowed around the whole land of Cush. **14** And the name of the third river is the Tigris, which flows east of Assyria. And the fourth river is the Euphrates.

15 The Lord God took the man and put him in the garden of Eden to work it and keep it. **16** And the Lord God commanded the man, saying, "You may surely eat of every tree of the garden, **17** but of the

tree of the knowledge of good and evil you shall not
eat, for in the day that you eat of it you shall surely
die."

---

*Use this time for other Advent observances: adding hay to the
Christmas Crib, hanging a new Jesse Tree ornament, or adding
figures to the Nativity Scene.*

The Lord's Prayer

All together
Our Father, who art in heaven,
hallowed be thy Name,
thy kingdom come, thy will be done,
on earth as it is in heaven.
Give us this day our daily bread.
And forgive us our trespasses,
as we forgive those who trespass against us.
And lead us not into temptation,
but deliver us from evil.
For thine is the kingdom,
and the power, and the glory,
for ever and ever. Amen.

The Blessing

Parents lay hands on each of your children and pray this blessing over them:

The Lord bless you and keep you. **Amen.**
The Lord make his face to shine upon you and be gracious to you. **Amen.**
The Lord lift up his countenance upon you and give you peace. **Amen.**

People: **Thanks be to God.**

DECEMBER 3

Start the devotion with the lights lowered or turned off.

Leader: Light and peace, in Jesus Christ our Lord.
People: **Thanks be to God.**
Leader: Let us pray.

If you are using the Great Advent Candle, light it at this time. If you are using an Advent Wreath, light the appropriate candles.

All together
O gracious light, pure brightness of the everliving
Father in heaven, O Jesus Christ, holy and blessed!
Now as we come to the setting of the sun, and our eyes
behold the vesper light, we sing your praises, O God:
Father, Son, and Holy Spirit.
You are worthy at all times to be praised by happy
voices, O Son of God, O Giver of Life,
and to be glorified through all the worlds.

A Reading From Holy Scripture

Read: Genesis 2:18-25

---

18 Then the Lord God said, "It is not good that the man should be alone; I will make him a helper fit for him." **19** Now out of the ground the Lord God had formed every beast of the field and every bird of the heavens and brought them to the man to see what he would call them. And whatever the man called every living creature, that was its name. **20** The man gave names to all livestock and to the birds of the heavens and to every beast of the field. But for Adam there was not found a helper fit for him. **21** So the Lord God caused a deep sleep to fall upon the man, and while he slept took one of his ribs and closed up its place with flesh. **22** And the rib that the Lord God had taken from the man he made into a woman and brought her to the man. **23** Then the man said, "This at last is bone of my bones and flesh of my flesh; she shall be called Woman, because she was taken out of Man." **24** Therefore a man shall leave his father and his mother and hold fast to his wife, and they shall become one flesh. **25** And the man and his wife were both naked and were not ashamed.

Use this time for other Advent observances: adding hay to the Christmas Crib, hanging a new Jesse Tree ornament, or adding figures to the Nativity Scene.

The Lord's Prayer

All together
Our Father, who art in heaven,
hallowed be thy Name,
thy kingdom come, thy will be done,
on earth as it is in heaven.
Give us this day our daily bread.
And forgive us our trespasses,
as we forgive those who trespass against us.
And lead us not into temptation,
but deliver us from evil.
For thine is the kingdom,
and the power, and the glory,
for ever and ever. Amen.

The Blessing

Parents lay hands on each of your children and pray this blessing over them:

The Lord bless you and keep you. **Amen.**
The Lord make his face to shine upon you and be gracious to you. **Amen.**
The Lord lift up his countenance upon you and give you peace. **Amen.**

People: **Thanks be to God.**

DECEMBER 4

Start the devotion with the lights lowered or turned off.

Leader: Light and peace, in Jesus Christ our Lord.
People: **Thanks be to God.**
Leader: Let us pray.

If you are using the Great Advent Candle, light it at this time. If you are using an Advent Wreath, light the appropriate candles.

All together
**O gracious light, pure brightness of the everliving
Father in heaven, O Jesus Christ, holy and blessed!
Now as we come to the setting of the sun, and our eyes
behold the vesper light, we sing your praises, O God:
Father, Son, and Holy Spirit.
You are worthy at all times to be praised by happy
voices, O Son of God, O Giver of Life,
and to be glorified through all the worlds.**

A Reading From Holy Scripture

Read: Genesis 3

---

3 Now the serpent was more crafty than any other
beast of the field that the Lord God had made. He
said to the woman, "Did God actually say, 'You
shall not eat of any tree in the garden'?" 2 And the

woman said to the serpent, "We may eat of the fruit of the trees in the garden, 3 but God said, 'You shall not eat of the fruit of the tree that is in the midst of the garden, neither shall you touch it, lest you die.'"

4 But the serpent said to the woman, "You will not surely die. 5 For God knows that when you eat of it your eyes will be opened, and you will be like God, knowing good and evil."

6 So when the woman saw that the tree was good for food, and that it was a delight to the eyes, and that the tree was to be desired to make one wise, she took of its fruit and ate, and she also gave some to her husband who was with her, and he ate. 7 Then the eyes of both were opened, and they knew that they were naked. And they sewed fig leaves together and made themselves loincloths.

8 And they heard the sound of the Lord God walking in the garden in the cool of the day, and the man and his wife hid themselves from the presence of the Lord God among the trees of the garden.

9 But the Lord God called to the man and said to him, "Where are you?" 10 And he said, "I heard the sound of you in the garden, and I was afraid, because I was naked, and I hid myself." 11 He said, "Who told you that you were naked? Have you eaten of the tree of which I commanded you not to eat?" 12 The man said, "The woman whom you gave to be

with me, she gave me fruit of the tree, and I ate." **13** Then the Lord God said to the woman, "What is this that you have done?" The woman said, "The serpent deceived me, and I ate."

14 The Lord God said to the serpent, "Because you have done this, cursed are you above all livestock and above all beasts of the field; on your belly you shall go, and dust you shall eat all the days of your life. **15** I will put enmity between you and the woman, and between your offspring and her offspring; he shall bruise your head, and you shall bruise his heel."

16 To the woman he said, "I will surely multiply your pain in childbearing; in pain you shall bring forth children. Your desire shall be contrary to your husband, but he shall rule over you." **17** And to Adam he said, "Because you have listened to the voice of your wife and have eaten of the tree of which I commanded you, 'You shall not eat of it,' cursed is the ground because of you; in pain you shall eat of it all the days of your life; **18** thorns and thistles it shall bring forth for you; and you shall eat the plants of the field. **19** By the sweat of your face you shall eat bread, till you return to the ground, for out of it you were taken; for you are dust, and to dust you shall return."

20 The man called his wife's name Eve, because she was the mother of all living. **21** And the Lord God made for Adam and for his wife garments of skins and clothed them.

22 Then the Lord God said, "Behold, the man has become like one of us in knowing good and evil. Now, lest he reach out his hand and take also of the tree of life and eat, and live forever" 23 therefore the Lord God sent him out from the garden of Eden to work the ground from which he was taken. 24 He drove out the man, and at the east of the garden of Eden he placed the cherubim and a flaming sword that turned every way to guard the way to the tree of life.

Use this time for other Advent observances: adding hay to the Christmas Crib, hanging a new Jesse Tree ornament, or adding figures to the Nativity Scene.

The Lord's Prayer

All together
Our Father, who art in heaven,
hallowed be thy Name,
thy kingdom come, thy will be done,
on earth as it is in heaven.
Give us this day our daily bread.
And forgive us our trespasses,
as we forgive those who trespass against us.
And lead us not into temptation,

but deliver us from evil.
For thine is the kingdom,
and the power, and the glory,
for ever and ever. Amen.

The Blessing

Parents lay hands on each of your children and pray this blessing over them:

The Lord bless you and keep you. **Amen.**
The Lord make his face to shine upon you and be gracious to you. **Amen.**
The Lord lift up his countenance upon you and give you peace. **Amen.**

People: **Thanks be to God.**

DECEMBER 5

Start the devotion with the lights lowered or turned off.

Leader: Light and peace, in Jesus Christ our Lord.
People: **Thanks be to God.**
Leader: Let us pray.

If you are using the Great Advent Candle, light it at this time. If you are using an Advent Wreath, light the appropriate candles.

All together
**O gracious light, pure brightness of the everliving
Father in heaven, O Jesus Christ, holy and blessed!
Now as we come to the setting of the sun, and our eyes
behold the vesper light, we sing your praises, O God:
Father, Son, and Holy Spirit.
You are worthy at all times to be praised by happy
voices, O Son of God, O Giver of Life,
and to be glorified through all the worlds.**

A Reading From Holy Scripture

Read: Genesis 12:1-5, 15:1-6

---

12 Now the Lord said to Abram, "Go from your country and your kindred and your father's house to the land that I will show you. **2** And I will make of you a great nation, and I will bless you and make your name great, so that you will be a blessing. **3** I will bless those who bless you, and him who dishonors you I will curse, and in you all the families of the earth shall be blessed."

4 So Abram went, as the Lord had told him, and Lot went with him. Abram was seventy-five years old when he departed from Haran. **5** And Abram took Sarai his wife, and Lot his brother's son, and all their possessions that they had gathered, and the people that they had acquired in Haran, and they set out to go to the land of Canaan.

Genesis 15:1-6

15 After these things the word of the Lord came to Abram in a vision: "Fear not, Abram, I am your shield; your reward shall be very great." **2** But Abram said, "O Lord God, what will you give me, for I continue childless, and the heir of my house is Eliezer of Damascus?" **3** And Abram said, "Behold, you have given me no offspring, and a member of my household will be my heir."

4 And behold, the word of the Lord came to him: "This man shall not be your heir; your very own son shall be your heir." **5** And he brought him outside and said, "Look toward heaven, and number the stars, if you are able to number them." Then he said to him, "So shall your offspring be."

6 And he believed the Lord, and he counted it to
him as righteousness.

---

*Use this time for other Advent observances: adding hay to the
Christmas Crib, hanging a new Jesse Tree ornament, or adding
figures to the Nativity Scene.*

The Lord's Prayer

All together
Our Father, who art in heaven,
hallowed be thy Name,
thy kingdom come, thy will be done,
on earth as it is in heaven.
Give us this day our daily bread.
And forgive us our trespasses,
as we forgive those who trespass against us.
And lead us not into temptation,
but deliver us from evil.
For thine is the kingdom,
and the power, and the glory,
for ever and ever. Amen.

The Blessing

Parents lay hands on each of your children and pray this blessing over them:

The Lord bless you and keep you. **Amen.**
The Lord make his face to shine upon you and be gracious to you. **Amen.**
The Lord lift up his countenance upon you and give you peace. **Amen.**

People: **Thanks be to God.**

DECEMBER 6

Start the devotion with the lights lowered or turned off.

Leader: Light and peace, in Jesus Christ our Lord.
People: **Thanks be to God.**
Leader: Let us pray.

If you are using the Great Advent Candle, light it at this time. If you are using an Advent Wreath, light the appropriate candles.

All together
O gracious light, pure brightness of the everliving
Father in heaven, O Jesus Christ, holy and blessed!
Now as we come to the setting of the sun, and our eyes
behold the vesper light, we sing your praises, O God:
Father, Son, and Holy Spirit.
You are worthy at all times to be praised by happy
voices, O Son of God, O Giver of Life,
and to be glorified through all the worlds.

A Reading From Holy Scripture

Read: Exodus 3:1-6

---

3 Now Moses was keeping the flock of his father-in-law, Jethro, the priest of Midian, and he led his flock to the west side of the wilderness and came to Horeb, the mountain of God. 2 And the angel of the

Lord appeared to him in a flame of fire out of the midst of a bush. He looked, and behold, the bush was burning, yet it was not consumed. 3 And Moses said, "I will turn aside to see this great sight, why the bush is not burned."

4 When the Lord saw that he turned aside to see, God called to him out of the bush, "Moses, Moses!" And he said, "Here I am." 5 Then he said, "Do not come near; take your sandals off your feet, for the place on which you are standing is holy ground." 6 And he said, "I am the God of your father, the God of Abraham, the God of Isaac, and the God of Jacob." And Moses hid his face, for he was afraid to look at God.

Use this time for other Advent observances: adding hay to the Christmas Crib, hanging a new Jesse Tree ornament, or adding figures to the Nativity Scene.

The Lord's Prayer

All together
Our Father, who art in heaven,
hallowed be thy Name,
thy kingdom come, thy will be done,
on earth as it is in heaven.
Give us this day our daily bread.
And forgive us our trespasses,

as we forgive those who trespass against us.
And lead us not into temptation,
but deliver us from evil.
For thine is the kingdom,
and the power, and the glory,
for ever and ever. Amen.

The Blessing

Parents lay hands on each of your children and pray this blessing over them:

The Lord bless you and keep you. **Amen.**
The Lord make his face to shine upon you and be gracious to you. **Amen.**
The Lord lift up his countenance upon you and give you peace. **Amen.**

People: **Thanks be to God.**

DECEMBER 7

Start the devotion with the lights lowered or turned off.

Leader: Light and peace, in Jesus Christ our Lord.
People: **Thanks be to God.**
Leader: Let us pray.

If you are using the Great Advent Candle, light it at this time. If you are using an Advent Wreath, light the appropriate candles.

All together
**O gracious light, pure brightness of the everliving
Father in heaven, O Jesus Christ, holy and blessed!
Now as we come to the setting of the sun, and our eyes
behold the vesper light, we sing your praises, O God:
Father, Son, and Holy Spirit.
You are worthy at all times to be praised by happy
voices, O Son of God, O Giver of Life,
and to be glorified through all the worlds.**

A Reading From Holy Scripture

Read: Exodus 12:1-14

---

12 The Lord said to Moses and Aaron in the land of
Egypt, **2** "This month shall be for you the beginning
of months. It shall be the first month of the year for
you. **3** Tell all the congregation of Israel that on the

tenth day of this month every man shall take a lamb according to their fathers' houses, a lamb for a household. 4 And if the household is too small for a lamb, then he and his nearest neighbor shall take according to the number of persons; according to what each can eat you shall make your count for the lamb. 5 Your lamb shall be without blemish, a male a year old. You may take it from the sheep or from the goats, 6 and you shall keep it until the fourteenth day of this month, when the whole assembly of the congregation of Israel shall kill their lambs at twilight. 7 "Then they shall take some of the blood and put it on the two doorposts and the lintel of the houses in which they eat it. 8 They shall eat the flesh that night, roasted on the fire; with unleavened bread and bitter herbs they shall eat it. 9 Do not eat any of it raw or boiled in water, but roasted, its head with its legs and its inner parts. 10 And you shall let none of it remain until the morning; anything that remains until the morning you shall burn.

11 In this manner you shall eat it: with your belt fastened, your sandals on your feet, and your staff in your hand. And you shall eat it in haste. It is the Lord's Passover. 12 For I will pass through the land of Egypt that night, and I will strike all the firstborn in the land of Egypt, both man and beast; and on all the gods of Egypt I will execute judgments: I am the Lord. 13 The blood shall be a sign for you, on the

houses where you are. And when I see the blood, I will pass over you, and no plague will befall you to destroy you, when I strike the land of Egypt. **14** "This day shall be for you a memorial day, and you shall keep it as a feast to the Lord; throughout your generations, as a statute forever, you shall keep it as a feast.

Use this time for other Advent observances: adding hay to the Christmas Crib, hanging a new Jesse Tree ornament, or adding figures to the Nativity Scene.

The Lord's Prayer

All together
Our Father, who art in heaven,
hallowed be thy Name,
thy kingdom come, thy will be done,
on earth as it is in heaven.
Give us this day our daily bread.
And forgive us our trespasses,
as we forgive those who trespass against us.
And lead us not into temptation,
but deliver us from evil.
For thine is the kingdom,
and the power, and the glory,
for ever and ever. Amen.

The Blessing

Parents lay hands on each of your children and pray this blessing over them:

The Lord bless you and keep you. **Amen.**
The Lord make his face to shine upon you and be gracious to you. **Amen.**
The Lord lift up his countenance upon you and give you peace. **Amen.**

People: **Thanks be to God.**

DECEMBER 8

Start the devotion with the lights lowered or turned off.

Leader: Light and peace, in Jesus Christ our Lord.
People: **Thanks be to God.**
Leader: Let us pray.

If you are using the Great Advent Candle, light it at this time. If you are using an Advent Wreath, light the appropriate candles.

All together
O gracious light, pure brightness of the everliving Father in heaven, O Jesus Christ, holy and blessed! Now as we come to the setting of the sun, and our eyes behold the vesper light, we sing your praises, O God: Father, Son, and Holy Spirit.
You are worthy at all times to be praised by happy voices, O Son of God, O Giver of Life, and to be glorified through all the worlds.

A Reading From Holy Scripture

Read: Exodus 14:10-31

---

10 When Pharaoh drew near, the people of Israel lifted up their eyes, and behold, the Egyptians were marching after them, and they feared greatly. And the people of Israel cried out to the Lord. **11** They said to Moses, "Is it because there are no graves in Egypt that you have taken us away to die in the wilderness? What have you done to us in bringing us out of Egypt? **12** Is not this what we said to you in Egypt: 'Leave us alone that we may serve the Egyptians'? For it would have been better for us to serve the Egyptians than to die in the wilderness." **13** And Moses said to the people, "Fear not, stand firm, and see the salvation of the Lord, which he will work for you today. For the Egyptians whom you see today, you shall never see again. **14** The Lord will fight for you, and you have only to be silent."

15 The Lord said to Moses, "Why do you cry to me? Tell the people of Israel to go forward. **16** Lift up your staff, and stretch out your hand over the sea and divide it, that the people of Israel may go through the sea on dry ground. **17** And I will harden the hearts of the Egyptians so that they shall go in after them, and I will get glory over Pharaoh and all his host, his chariots, and his horsemen. **18** And the Egyptians shall know that I am the Lord, when I have gotten glory over Pharaoh, his chariots, and his horsemen."

19 Then the angel of God who was going before the host of Israel moved and went behind them, and the pillar of cloud moved from before them and stood behind them, **20** coming between the host of Egypt and the host of Israel. And there was the cloud and the darkness. And it lit up the night without one coming near the other all night.

21 Then Moses stretched out his hand over the sea, and the Lord drove the sea back by a strong east wind all night and made the sea dry land, and the waters were divided. 22 And the people of Israel went into the midst of the sea on dry ground, the waters being a wall to them on their right hand and on their left. 23 The Egyptians pursued and went in after them into the midst of the sea, all Pharaoh's horses, his chariots, and his horsemen. 24 And in the morning watch the Lord in the pillar of fire and of cloud looked down on the Egyptian forces and threw the Egyptian forces into a panic, 25 clogging their chariot wheels so that they drove heavily. And the Egyptians said, "Let us flee from before Israel, for the Lord fights for them against the Egyptians."

26 Then the Lord said to Moses, "Stretch out your hand over the sea, that the water may come back upon the Egyptians, upon their chariots, and upon their horsemen." 27 So Moses stretched out his hand over the sea, and the sea returned to its normal course when the morning appeared. And as the Egyptians fled into it, the Lord threw the Egyptians into the midst of the sea. 28 The waters returned and covered the chariots and the horsemen; of all the host of Pharaoh that had followed them into the sea, not one of them remained. 29 But the people of

Israel walked on dry ground through the sea, the waters being a wall to them on their right hand and on their left. **30** Thus the Lord saved Israel that day from the hand of the Egyptians, and Israel saw the Egyptians dead on the seashore. **31** Israel saw the great power that the Lord used against the Egyptians, so the people feared the Lord, and they believed in the Lord and in his servant Moses.

Use this time for other Advent observances: adding hay to the Christmas Crib, hanging a new Jesse Tree ornament, or adding figures to the Nativity Scene.

The Lord's Prayer

All together
**Our Father, who art in heaven,
hallowed be thy Name,
thy kingdom come, thy will be done,
on earth as it is in heaven.
Give us this day our daily bread.
And forgive us our trespasses,
as we forgive those who trespass against us.
And lead us not into temptation,
but deliver us from evil.
For thine is the kingdom,
and the power, and the glory,
for ever and ever. Amen.**

The Blessing

Parents lay hands on each of your children and pray this blessing over them:

The Lord bless you and keep you. **Amen.**
The Lord make his face to shine upon you and be gracious to you. **Amen.**
The Lord lift up his countenance upon you and give you peace. **Amen.**

People: **Thanks be to God.**

DECEMBER 9

Start the devotion with the lights lowered or turned off.

Leader: Light and peace, in Jesus Christ our Lord.
People: **Thanks be to God.**
Leader: Let us pray.

If you are using the Great Advent Candle, light it at this time. If you are using an Advent Wreath, light the appropriate candles.

All together
O gracious light, pure brightness of the everliving
Father in heaven, O Jesus Christ, holy and blessed!
Now as we come to the setting of the sun, and our eyes
behold the vesper light, we sing your praises, O God:
Father, Son, and Holy Spirit.
You are worthy at all times to be praised by happy
voices, O Son of God, O Giver of Life,
and to be glorified through all the worlds.

A Reading From Holy Scripture

Read: Ruth 1:1-22, 4:13-17

---

1 In the days when the judges ruled there was a famine in the land, and a man of Bethlehem in Judah went to sojourn in the country of Moab, he and his wife and his two sons. 2 The name of the man was

Elimelech and the name of his wife Naomi, and the names of his two sons were Mahlon and Chilion. They were Ephrathites from Bethlehem in Judah. They went into the country of Moab and remained there. 3 But Elimelech, the husband of Naomi, died, and she was left with her two sons. 4 These took Moabite wives; the name of the one was Orpah and the name of the other Ruth. They lived there about ten years, 5 and both Mahlon and Chilion died, so that the woman was left without her two sons and her husband.

6 Then she arose with her daughters-in-law to return from the country of Moab, for she had heard in the fields of Moab that the Lord had visited his people and given them food. 7 So she set out from the place where she was with her two daughters-in-law, and they went on the way to return to the land of Judah. 8 But Naomi said to her two daughters-in-law, "Go, return each of you to her mother's house. May the Lord deal kindly with you, as you have dealt with the dead and with me. 9 The Lord grant that you may find rest, each of you in the house of her husband!" Then she kissed them, and they lifted up their voices and wept. 10 And they said to her, "No, we will return with you to your people." 11 But Naomi said, "Turn back, my daughters; why will you go with me? Have I yet sons in my womb that they may become your husbands? 12 Turn back, my daughters; go your

way, for I am too old to have a husband. If I should say I have hope, even if I should have a husband this night and should bear sons, **13** would you therefore wait till they were grown? Would you therefore refrain from marrying? No, my daughters, for it is exceedingly bitter to me for your sake that the hand of the Lord has gone out against me." **14** Then they lifted up their voices and wept again. And Orpah kissed her mother-in-law, but Ruth clung to her.

15 And she said, "See, your sister-in-law has gone back to her people and to her gods; return after your sister-in-law." **16** But Ruth said, "Do not urge me to leave you or to return from following you. For where you go I will go, and where you lodge I will lodge. Your people shall be my people, and your God my God. **17** Where you die I will die, and there will I be buried. May the Lord do so to me and more also if anything but death parts me from you." **18** And when Naomi saw that she was determined to go with her, she said no more.

19 So the two of them went on until they came to Bethlehem. And when they came to Bethlehem, the whole town was stirred because of them. And the women said, "Is this Naomi?" **20** She said to them, "Do not call me Naomi; call me Mara, for the Almighty has dealt very bitterly with me. **21** I went away full, and the Lord has brought me back empty. Why call me Naomi, when the Lord has testified against me and the Almighty has brought calamity upon me?"

22 So Naomi returned, and Ruth the Moabite her daughter-in-law with her, who returned from the country of Moab. And they came to Bethlehem at the beginning of barley harvest.

Ruth 4:13-17

13 So Boaz took Ruth, and she became his wife. And he went in to her, and the Lord gave her conception, and she bore a son. **14** Then the women said to Naomi, "Blessed be the Lord, who has not left you this day without a redeemer, and may his name be renowned in Israel! **15** He shall be to you a restorer of life and a nourisher of your old age, for your daughter-in-law who loves you, who is more to you than seven sons, has given birth to him." **16** Then Naomi took the child and laid him on her lap and became his nurse. **17** And the women of the neighborhood gave him a name, saying, "A son has been born to Naomi." They named him Obed. He was the father of Jesse, the father of David.

Use this time for other Advent observances: adding hay to the Christmas Crib, hanging a new Jesse Tree ornament, or adding figures to the Nativity Scene.

The Lord's Prayer

All together
Our Father, who art in heaven,
hallowed be thy Name,
thy kingdom come, thy will be done,
on earth as it is in heaven.
Give us this day our daily bread.
And forgive us our trespasses,
as we forgive those who trespass against us.
And lead us not into temptation,
but deliver us from evil.
For thine is the kingdom,
and the power, and the glory,
for ever and ever. Amen.

The Blessing

Parents lay hands on each of your children and pray this blessing over them:

The Lord bless you and keep you. **Amen.**
The Lord make his face to shine upon you and be gracious to you. **Amen.**
The Lord lift up his countenance upon you and give you peace. **Amen.**

People: **Thanks be to God.**

DECEMBER 10

Start the devotion with the lights lowered or turned off.

Leader: Light and peace, in Jesus Christ our Lord.
People: **Thanks be to God.**
Leader: Let us pray.

If you are using the Great Advent Candle, light it at this time. If you are using an Advent Wreath, light the appropriate candles.

All together
O gracious light, pure brightness of the everliving
Father in heaven, O Jesus Christ, holy and blessed!
Now as we come to the setting of the sun, and our eyes
behold the vesper light, we sing your praises, O God:
Father, Son, and Holy Spirit.
You are worthy at all times to be praised by happy
voices, O Son of God, O Giver of Life,
and to be glorified through all the worlds.

A Reading From Holy Scripture

Read: 1 Samuel 1:1-28

---

1 There was a certain man of Ramathaim-zophim of the hill country of Ephraim whose name was Elkanah the son of Jeroham, son of Elihu, son of Tohu, son of Zuph, an Ephrathite. **2** He had two wives. The name of the one was Hannah, and the name of the other, Peninnah. And Peninnah had children, but Hannah had no children.

3 Now this man used to go up year by year from his city to worship and to sacrifice to the Lord of hosts at Shiloh, where the two sons of Eli, Hophni and Phinehas, were priests of the Lord. 4 On the day when Elkanah sacrificed, he would give portions to Peninnah his wife and to all her sons and daughters. 5 But to Hannah he gave a double portion, because he loved her, though the Lord had closed her womb. 6 And her rival used to provoke her grievously to irritate her, because the Lord had closed her womb. 7 So it went on year by year. As often as she went up to the house of the Lord, she used to provoke her. Therefore Hannah wept and would not eat. 8 And Elkanah, her husband, said to her, "Hannah, why do you weep? And why do you not eat? And why is your heart sad? Am I not more to you than ten sons?"

9 After they had eaten and drunk in Shiloh, Hannah rose. Now Eli the priest was sitting on the seat beside the doorpost of the temple of the Lord. 10 She was deeply distressed and prayed to the Lord and wept bitterly. 11 And she vowed a vow and said, "O Lord of hosts, if you will indeed look on the affliction of your servant and remember me and not forget your servant, but will give to your servant a

son, then I will give him to the Lord all the days of his life, and no razor shall touch his head."

12 As she continued praying before the Lord, Eli observed her mouth. 13 Hannah was speaking in her heart; only her lips moved, and her voice was not heard. Therefore Eli took her to be a drunken woman. 14 And Eli said to her, "How long will you go on being drunk? Put your wine away from you." 15 But Hannah answered, "No, my lord, I am a woman troubled in spirit. I have drunk neither wine nor strong drink, but I have been pouring out my soul before the Lord. 16 Do not regard your servant as a worthless woman, for all along I have been speaking out of my great anxiety and vexation." 17 Then Eli answered, "Go in peace, and the God of Israel grant your petition that you have made to him." 18 And she said, "Let your servant find favor in your eyes." Then the woman went her way and ate, and her face was no longer sad.

19 They rose early in the morning and worshiped before the Lord; then they went back to their house at Ramah. And Elkanah knew Hannah his wife, and the Lord remembered her. 20 And in due time Hannah conceived and bore a son, and she called his name Samuel, for she said, "I have asked for him from the Lord."

21 The man Elkanah and all his house went up to offer to the Lord the yearly sacrifice and to pay his

vow. **22** But Hannah did not go up, for she said to her husband, "As soon as the child is weaned, I will bring him, so that he may appear in the presence of the Lord and dwell there forever." **23** Elkanah her husband said to her, "Do what seems best to you; wait until you have weaned him; only, may the Lord establish his word." So the woman remained and nursed her son until she weaned him. **24** And when she had weaned him, she took him up with her, along with a three-year-old bull, an ephah of flour, and a skin of wine, and she brought him to the house of the Lord at Shiloh. And the child was young. **25** Then they slaughtered the bull, and they brought the child to Eli. **26** And she said, "Oh, my lord! As you live, my lord, I am the woman who was standing here in your presence, praying to the Lord. **27** For this child I prayed, and the Lord has granted me my petition that I made to him. **28** Therefore I have lent him to the Lord. As long as he lives, he is lent to the Lord." And he worshiped the Lord there.

Use this time for other Advent observances: adding hay to the Christmas Crib, hanging a new Jesse Tree ornament, or adding figures to the Nativity Scene.

The Lord's Prayer

All together
**Our Father, who art in heaven,
hallowed be thy Name,
thy kingdom come, thy will be done,
on earth as it is in heaven.
Give us this day our daily bread.
And forgive us our trespasses,
as we forgive those who trespass against us.
And lead us not into temptation,
but deliver us from evil.
For thine is the kingdom,
and the power, and the glory,
for ever and ever. Amen.**

The Blessing

*Parents lay hands on each of your children and pray this
blessing over them:*

The Lord bless you and keep you. **Amen.**
The Lord make his face to shine upon you and be gracious
to you. **Amen.**
The Lord lift up his countenance upon you and give you
peace. **Amen.**

People: **Thanks be to God.**

DECEMBER 11

Start the devotion with the lights lowered or turned off.

Leader: Light and peace, in Jesus Christ our Lord.
People: **Thanks be to God.**
Leader: Let us pray.

If you are using the Great Advent Candle, light it at this time. If you are using an Advent Wreath, light the appropriate candles.

All together
**O gracious light, pure brightness of the everliving
Father in heaven, O Jesus Christ, holy and blessed!
Now as we come to the setting of the sun, and our eyes
behold the vesper light, we sing your praises, O God:
Father, Son, and Holy Spirit.
You are worthy at all times to be praised by happy
voices, O Son of God, O Giver of Life,
and to be glorified through all the worlds.**

A Reading From Holy Scripture

Read: 1 Samuel 2:1-11 (ESV)

---

2 And Hannah prayed and said, "My heart exults in the Lord; my horn is exalted in the Lord. My mouth derides my enemies, because I rejoice in your salvation. 2 "There is none holy like the Lord: for

there is none besides you; there is no rock like our God. 3 Talk no more so very proudly, let not arrogance come from your mouth; for the Lord is a God of knowledge, and by him actions are weighed. 4 The bows of the mighty are broken, but the feeble bind on strength. 5 Those who were full have hired themselves out for bread, but those who were hungry have ceased to hunger. The barren has borne seven, but she who has many children is forlorn. 6 The Lord kills and brings to life; he brings down to Sheol and raises up. 7 The Lord makes poor and makes rich; he brings low and he exalts. 8 He raises up the poor from the dust; he lifts the needy from the ash heap to make them sit with princes and inherit a seat of honor. For the pillars of the earth are the Lord's, and on them he has set the world. 9 "He will guard the feet of his faithful ones, but the wicked shall be cut off in darkness, for not by might shall a man prevail. 10 The adversaries of the Lord shall be broken to pieces; against them he will thunder in heaven. The Lord will judge the ends of the earth; he will give strength to his king and exalt the horn of his anointed."

11 Then Elkanah went home to Ramah. And the boy was ministering to the Lord in the presence of Eli the priest.

Use this time for other Advent observances: adding hay to the Christmas Crib, hanging a new Jesse Tree ornament, or adding figures to the Nativity Scene.

The Lord's Prayer

All together
**Our Father, who art in heaven,
hallowed be thy Name,
thy kingdom come, thy will be done,
on earth as it is in heaven.
Give us this day our daily bread.
And forgive us our trespasses,
as we forgive those who trespass against us.
And lead us not into temptation,
but deliver us from evil.
For thine is the kingdom,
and the power, and the glory,
for ever and ever. Amen.**

The Blessing

Parents lay hands on each of your children and pray this blessing over them:

The Lord bless you and keep you. **Amen.**
The Lord make his face to shine upon you and be gracious to you. **Amen.**
The Lord lift up his countenance upon you and give you peace. **Amen.**

People: **Thanks be to God.**

DECEMBER 12

Start the devotion with the lights lowered or turned off.

Leader: Light and peace, in Jesus Christ our Lord.
People: **Thanks be to God.**
Leader: Let us pray.

If you are using the Great Advent Candle, light it at this time. If you are using an Advent Wreath, light the appropriate candles.

All together
**O gracious light, pure brightness of the everliving
Father in heaven, O Jesus Christ, holy and blessed!
Now as we come to the setting of the sun, and our eyes
behold the vesper light, we sing your praises, O God:
Father, Son, and Holy Spirit.
You are worthy at all times to be praised by happy
voices, O Son of God, O Giver of Life,
and to be glorified through all the worlds.**

A Reading From Holy Scripture

Read: Isaiah 60:1-3 (ESV)

---

1 Arise, shine, for your light has come, and the glory of the Lord has risen upon you. 2 For behold, darkness shall cover the earth, and thick darkness the peoples; but the Lord will arise upon you, and

his glory will be seen upon you. 3 And nations shall come to your light, and kings to the brightness of your rising.

Use this time for other Advent observances: adding hay to the Christmas Crib, hanging a new Jesse Tree ornament, or adding figures to the Nativity Scene.

The Lord's Prayer

All together
Our Father, who art in heaven,
hallowed be thy Name,
thy kingdom come, thy will be done,
on earth as it is in heaven.
Give us this day our daily bread.
And forgive us our trespasses,
as we forgive those who trespass against us.
And lead us not into temptation,
but deliver us from evil.
For thine is the kingdom,
and the power, and the glory,
for ever and ever. Amen.

The Blessing

Parents lay hands on each of your children and pray this blessing over them:

The Lord bless you and keep you. **Amen**.
The Lord make his face to shine upon you and be gracious to you. **Amen**.
The Lord lift up his countenance upon you and give you peace. **Amen**.

People: **Thanks be to God.**

DECEMBER 13

Start the devotion with the lights lowered or turned off.

Leader: Light and peace, in Jesus Christ our Lord.
People: **Thanks be to God.**
Leader: Let us pray.

If you are using the Great Advent Candle, light it at this time. If you are using an Advent Wreath, light the appropriate candles.

All together
**O gracious light, pure brightness of the everliving
Father in heaven, O Jesus Christ, holy and blessed!
Now as we come to the setting of the sun, and our eyes
behold the vesper light, we sing your praises, O God:
Father, Son, and Holy Spirit.
You are worthy at all times to be praised by happy
voices, O Son of God, O Giver of Life,
and to be glorified through all the worlds.**

A Reading From Holy Scripture

Read: Isaiah 9:2 (ESV)

---

2 The people who walked in darkness have seen a great light; those who dwelt in a land of deep darkness, on them has light shone.

Use this time for other Advent observances: adding hay to the Christmas Crib, hanging a new Jesse Tree ornament, or adding figures to the Nativity Scene.

The Lord's Prayer

All together
Our Father, who art in heaven,
hallowed be thy Name,
thy kingdom come, thy will be done,
on earth as it is in heaven.
Give us this day our daily bread.
And forgive us our trespasses,
as we forgive those who trespass against us.
And lead us not into temptation,
but deliver us from evil.
For thine is the kingdom,
and the power, and the glory,
for ever and ever. Amen.

The Blessing

Parents lay hands on each of your children and pray this blessing over them:

The Lord bless you and keep you. **Amen.**
The Lord make his face to shine upon you and be gracious to you. **Amen.**
The Lord lift up his countenance upon you and give you peace. **Amen.**

People: **Thanks be to God.**

DECEMBER 14

Start the devotion with the lights lowered or turned off.

Leader: Light and peace, in Jesus Christ our Lord.
People: **Thanks be to God.**
Leader: Let us pray.

If you are using the Great Advent Candle, light it at this time. If you are using an Advent Wreath, light the appropriate candles.

All together
**O gracious light, pure brightness of the everliving
Father in heaven, O Jesus Christ, holy and blessed!
Now as we come to the setting of the sun, and our eyes
behold the vesper light, we sing your praises, O God:
Father, Son, and Holy Spirit.
You are worthy at all times to be praised by happy
voices, O Son of God, O Giver of Life,
and to be glorified through all the worlds.**

A Reading From Holy Scripture

Read: Isaiah 35:5-6

---

5 And when he comes, he will open the eyes of the blind and unplug the ears of the deaf. 6 The lame will leap like a deer, and those who cannot speak

will sing for joy! Springs will gush forth in the wilderness, and streams will water the wasteland.

Use this time for other Advent observances: adding hay to the Christmas Crib, hanging a new Jesse Tree ornament, or adding figures to the Nativity Scene.

The Lord's Prayer

All together
Our Father, who art in heaven,
hallowed be thy Name,
thy kingdom come, thy will be done,
on earth as it is in heaven.
Give us this day our daily bread.
And forgive us our trespasses,
as we forgive those who trespass against us.
And lead us not into temptation,
but deliver us from evil.
For thine is the kingdom,
and the power, and the glory,
for ever and ever. Amen.

The Blessing

Parents lay hands on each of your children and pray this blessing over them:

The Lord bless you and keep you. **Amen.**
The Lord make his face to shine upon you and be gracious to you. **Amen.**
The Lord lift up his countenance upon you and give you peace. **Amen.**

People: **Thanks be to God.**

DECEMBER 15

Start the devotion with the lights lowered or turned off.

Leader: Light and peace, in Jesus Christ our Lord.
People: **Thanks be to God.**
Leader: Let us pray.

If you are using the Great Advent Candle, light it at this time. If you are using an Advent Wreath, light the appropriate candles.

All together
O gracious light, pure brightness of the everliving Father in heaven, O Jesus Christ, holy and blessed! Now as we come to the setting of the sun, and our eyes behold the vesper light, we sing your praises, O God: Father, Son, and Holy Spirit.
You are worthy at all times to be praised by happy voices, O Son of God, O Giver of Life, and to be glorified through all the worlds.

A Reading From Holy Scripture

Read: Isaiah 40:9,11

---

9 O Zion, messenger of good news, shout from the mountaintops! Shout it louder, O Jerusalem, Shout, and do not be afraid. Tell the towns of Judah, "Your God is coming!"

11 He will feed his flock like a shepherd. He will carry the lambs in his arms, holding them close to his heart. He will gently lead the mother sheep with their young.

Use this time for other Advent observances: adding hay to the Christmas Crib, hanging a new Jesse Tree ornament, or adding figures to the Nativity Scene.

The Lord's Prayer

All together
**Our Father, who art in heaven,
hallowed be thy Name,
thy kingdom come, thy will be done,
on earth as it is in heaven.
Give us this day our daily bread.
And forgive us our trespasses,
as we forgive those who trespass against us.
And lead us not into temptation,
but deliver us from evil.
For thine is the kingdom,
and the power, and the glory,
for ever and ever. Amen.**

The Blessing

Parents lay hands on each of your children and pray this blessing over them:

The Lord bless you and keep you. **Amen.**
The Lord make his face to shine upon you and be gracious to you. **Amen.**
The Lord lift up his countenance upon you and give you peace. **Amen.**

People: **Thanks be to God.**

DECEMBER 16

Start the devotion with the lights lowered or turned off.

Leader: Light and peace, in Jesus Christ our Lord.
People: **Thanks be to God.**
Leader: Let us pray.

If you are using the Great Advent Candle, light it at this time. If you are using an Advent Wreath, light the appropriate candles.

All together
**O gracious light, pure brightness of the everliving
Father in heaven, O Jesus Christ, holy and blessed!
Now as we come to the setting of the sun, and our eyes
behold the vesper light, we sing your praises, O God:
Father, Son, and Holy Spirit.
You are worthy at all times to be praised by happy
voices, O Son of God, O Giver of Life,
and to be glorified through all the worlds.**

A Reading From Holy Scripture

Read: Isaiah 40:1-5 (ESV)

---

1 Comfort, comfort my people, says your God. 2 Speak tenderly to Jerusalem, and cry to her that her warfare is ended, that her iniquity is pardoned, that she has received from the Lord's hand double for all

her sins. 3 A voice cries:"In the wilderness prepare the way of the Lord; make straight in the desert a highway for our God. 4 Every valley shall be lifted up, and every mountain and hill be made low; the uneven ground shall become level, and the rough places a plain. 5 And the glory of the Lord shall be revealed, and all flesh shall see it together, for the mouth of the Lord has spoken."

Today marks the beginning of the Novena (nine days) or countdown to Christmas Day. It is the day that La Posada or Golden Nights begins. See the La Posada section of the book in Chapter 5 for the history of the day and ways to celebrate.

Use this time for other Advent observances: adding hay to the Christmas Crib, hanging a new Jesse Tree ornament, or adding figures to the Nativity Scene.

The Lord's Prayer

All together
Our Father, who art in heaven,
hallowed be thy Name,
thy kingdom come, thy will be done,
on earth as it is in heaven.
Give us this day our daily bread.
And forgive us our trespasses,
as we forgive those who trespass against us.
And lead us not into temptation,

but deliver us from evil.
For thine is the kingdom,
and the power, and the glory,
for ever and ever. Amen.

The Blessing

Parents lay hands on each of your children and pray this blessing over them:

The Lord bless you and keep you. **Amen**.
The Lord make his face to shine upon you and be gracious to you. **Amen**.
The Lord lift up his countenance upon you and give you peace. **Amen**.

People: **Thanks be to God.**

DECEMBER 17

Start the devotion with the lights lowered or turned off.

Leader: Light and peace, in Jesus Christ our Lord.
People: **Thanks be to God.**
Leader: Let us pray.

If you are using the Great Advent Candle, light it at this time. If you are using an Advent Wreath, light the appropriate candles.

All together
O gracious light, pure brightness of the everliving Father in heaven, O Jesus Christ, holy and blessed! Now as we come to the setting of the sun, and our eyes behold the vesper light, we sing your praises, O God: Father, Son, and Holy Spirit.
You are worthy at all times to be praised by happy voices, O Son of God, O Giver of Life, and to be glorified through all the worlds.

A Reading From Holy Scripture

Read: Isaiah 7:14

---

14 Therefore the Lord himself will give you a sign. Behold, the virgin shall conceive and bear a son, and shall call his name Immanuel.

Use this time for other Advent observances: adding hay to the Christmas Crib, hanging a new Jesse Tree ornament, or adding figures to the Nativity Scene.

Continue any Novena *(nine days)*, La Posada *or* Golden Nights *celebrations. See the "La Posada" section of the book in Chapter 5 for the history of the day and ways to celebrate.*

Today also marks the beginning of the Octave *(eight days) or countdown to Christmas Day. It is the day that the "O Antiphons" begin. See the "O Antiphons" section of the book for the history and ways to celebrate.*

Sing the "O Antiphon" for the day:

**"O come, O come, Emmanuel,
and ransom captive Israel,
that mourns in lonely exile here
until the Son of God appear.
Rejoice! Rejoice!
Emmanuel shall come to thee, O Israel!**

**O come, thou Wisdom from on high,
who orderest all things mightily;
to us the path of knowledge show,
and teach us in her ways to go.
Rejoice! Rejoice!
Emmanuel shall come to thee, O Israel!"**

The Lord's Prayer

All together
**Our Father, who art in heaven,
hallowed be thy Name,
thy kingdom come, thy will be done,
on earth as it is in heaven.
Give us this day our daily bread.
And forgive us our trespasses,
as we forgive those who trespass against us.
And lead us not into temptation,
but deliver us from evil.
For thine is the kingdom,
and the power, and the glory,
for ever and ever. Amen.**

The Blessing

Parents lay hands on each of your children and pray this blessing over them:

The Lord bless you and keep you. **Amen.**
The Lord make his face to shine upon you and be gracious to you. **Amen.**
The Lord lift up his countenance upon you and give you peace. **Amen.**

People: **Thanks be to God.**

DECEMBER 18

Start the devotion with the lights lowered or turned off.

Leader: Light and peace, in Jesus Christ our Lord.
People: **Thanks be to God.**
Leader: Let us pray.

If you are using the Great Advent Candle, light it at this time. If you are using an Advent Wreath, light the appropriate candles.

All together
O gracious light, pure brightness of the everliving
Father in heaven, O Jesus Christ, holy and blessed!
Now as we come to the setting of the sun, and our eyes
behold the vesper light, we sing your praises, O God:
Father, Son, and Holy Spirit.
You are worthy at all times to be praised by happy
voices, O Son of God, O Giver of Life,
and to be glorified through all the worlds.

A Reading From Holy Scripture

Read: Isaiah 9:6 (ESV)

---

6 For unto us a child is born, to us a son is given;
and the government shall be upon his shoulder, and
his name shall be called Wonderful Counselor,
Mighty God, Everlasting Father, Prince of Peace.

Use this time for other Advent observances: adding hay to the Christmas Crib, hanging a new Jesse Tree ornament, or adding figures to the Nativity Scene.

Continue any Novena (nine days), La Posada or Golden Nights celebrations. See the "La Posada" section of the book in Chapter 5 for the history of the day and ways to celebrate.

Continue singing the "O Antiphons" for the day. See the "O Antiphons" section of the book for the history and ways to celebrate.

Sing the "O Antiphon" for the day:

**"O come, O come, Emmanuel,
and ransom captive Israel,
that mourns in lonely exile here
until the Son of God appear.
Rejoice! Rejoice!
Emmanuel shall come to thee, O Israel!**

**O come, thou Rod of Jesse, free
thine own from Satan's tyranny;
from depths of hell thy people save,
and give them victory over the grave.
Rejoice! Rejoice!
Emmanuel shall come to thee, O Israel!"**

The Lord's Prayer

All together
**Our Father, who art in heaven,
hallowed be thy Name,
thy kingdom come, thy will be done,
on earth as it is in heaven.
Give us this day our daily bread.
And forgive us our trespasses,
as we forgive those who trespass against us.
And lead us not into temptation,
but deliver us from evil.
For thine is the kingdom,
and the power, and the glory,
for ever and ever. Amen.**

The Blessing

Parents lay hands on each of your children and pray this blessing over them:

The Lord bless you and keep you. **Amen.**
The Lord make his face to shine upon you and be gracious to you. **Amen.**
The Lord lift up his countenance upon you and give you peace. **Amen.**

People: **Thanks be to God.**

DECEMBER 19

Start the devotion with the lights lowered or turned off.

Leader: Light and peace, in Jesus Christ our Lord.
People: **Thanks be to God.**
Leader: Let us pray.

If you are using the Great Advent Candle, light it at this time. If you are using an Advent Wreath, light the appropriate candles.

All together
O gracious light, pure brightness of the everliving Father in heaven, O Jesus Christ, holy and blessed! Now as we come to the setting of the sun, and our eyes behold the vesper light, we sing your praises, O God: Father, Son, and Holy Spirit.
You are worthy at all times to be praised by happy voices, O Son of God, O Giver of Life,
and to be glorified through all the worlds.

A Reading From Holy Scripture

Read: Luke 1:5-25 (ESV)

---

5 In the days of Herod, king of Judea, there was a priest named Zechariah, of the division of Abijah. And he had a wife from the daughters of Aaron, and

her name was Elizabeth. **6** And they were both righteous before God, walking blamelessly in all the commandments and statutes of the Lord. **7** But they had no child, because Elizabeth was barren, and both were advanced in years.

8 Now while he was serving as priest before God when his division was on duty, **9** according to the custom of the priesthood, he was chosen by lot to enter the temple of the Lord and burn incense. **10** And the whole multitude of the people were praying outside at the hour of incense. **11** And there appeared to him an angel of the Lord standing on the right side of the altar of incense. **12** And Zechariah was troubled when he saw him, and fear fell upon him. **13** But the angel said to him, "Do not be afraid, Zechariah, for your prayer has been heard, and your wife Elizabeth will bear you a son, and you shall call his name John. **14** And you will have joy and gladness, and many will rejoice at his birth, **15** for he will be great before the Lord. And he must not drink wine or strong drink, and he will be filled with the Holy Spirit, even from his mother's womb. **16** And he will turn many of the children of Israel to the Lord their God, **17** and he will go before him in the spirit and power of Elijah, to turn the hearts of the fathers to the children, and the disobedient to the wisdom of the just, to make ready for the Lord a people prepared."

18 And Zechariah said to the angel, "How shall I know this? For I am an old man, and my wife is advanced in years." **19** And the angel answered him, "I am Gabriel. I stand in the presence of God, and I was sent to speak to you and to bring you this good news. **20** And behold, you will be silent and unable to speak until the day that these things take place, because you did not believe my words, which will be fulfilled in their time." **21** And the people were waiting for Zechariah, and they were wondering at his delay in the temple. **22** And when he came out, he was unable to speak to them, and they realized that he had seen a vision in the temple. And he kept making signs to them and remained mute. **23** And when his time of service was ended, he went to his home.

24 After these days his wife Elizabeth conceived, and for five months she kept herself hidden, saying, **25** "Thus the Lord has done for me in the days when he looked on me, to take away my reproach among people."

Use this time for other Advent observances: adding hay to the Christmas Crib, hanging a new Jesse Tree ornament, or adding figures to the Nativity Scene.

Continue any Novena (nine days), La Posada or Golden Nights celebrations. See the "La Posada" section of the book in Chapter 5 for the history of the day and ways to celebrate.

Continue singing the "O Antiphons" for the day. See the "O Antiphons" section of the book for the history and ways to celebrate.

Sing the O' Antiphon for the day:

"O come, O come, Emmanuel,
and ransom captive Israel,
that mourns in lonely exile here
until the Son of God appear.
Rejoice! Rejoice!
Emmanuel shall come to thee, O Israel!

O come, thou Dayspring, come and cheer
our spirits by thine advent here;
disperse the gloomy clouds of night,
and death's dark shadow put to flight.
Rejoice! Rejoice!
Emmanuel shall come to thee, O Israel!"

The Lord's Prayer

All together
Our Father, who art in heaven,
hallowed be thy Name,
thy kingdom come, thy will be done,
on earth as it is in heaven.
Give us this day our daily bread.
And forgive us our trespasses,
as we forgive those who trespass against us.
And lead us not into temptation,
but deliver us from evil.
For thine is the kingdom,
and the power, and the glory,
for ever and ever. Amen.

The Blessing

Parents lay hands on each of your children and pray this blessing over them:

The Lord bless you and keep you. **Amen.**
The Lord make his face to shine upon you and be gracious to you. **Amen.**
The Lord lift up his countenance upon you and give you peace. **Amen.**

People: **Thanks be to God.**

DECEMBER 20

Start the devotion with the lights lowered or turned off.

Leader: Light and peace, in Jesus Christ our Lord.
People: **Thanks be to God.**
Leader: Let us pray.

If you are using the Great Advent Candle, light it at this time. If you are using an Advent Wreath, light the appropriate candles.

All together
**O gracious light, pure brightness of the everliving
Father in heaven, O Jesus Christ, holy and blessed!
Now as we come to the setting of the sun, and our eyes
behold the vesper light, we sing your praises, O God:
Father, Son, and Holy Spirit.
You are worthy at all times to be praised by happy
voices, O Son of God, O Giver of Life,
and to be glorified through all the worlds.**

A Reading From Holy Scripture

Read: Matthew 1:18-25 (ESV)

---

18 Now the birth of Jesus Christ took place in this way. When his mother Mary had been betrothed to Joseph, before they came together she was found to be with child from the Holy Spirit. **19** And her husband Joseph, being a just man and unwilling to put her to shame, resolved to divorce her quietly. **20** But as he considered these things, behold, an angel of the Lord appeared to him in a dream, saying, "Joseph, son of David, do not fear to take Mary as your wife, for that which is conceived in her is from the Holy Spirit. **21** She will bear a son, and you shall call his name Jesus, for he will save his people from their sins." **22** All this took place to fulfill what the Lord had spoken by the prophet:

23 "Behold, the virgin shall conceive and bear a son, and they shall call his name Immanuel" (which means, God with us). **24** When Joseph woke from sleep, he did as the angel of the Lord commanded him: he took his wife, **25** but knew her not until she had given birth to a son. And he called his name Jesus.

Use this time for other Advent observances: adding hay to the Christmas Crib, hanging a new Jesse Tree ornament, or adding figures to the Nativity Scene.

Continue any Novena (nine days), La Posada or Golden Nights celebrations. See the "La Posada" section of the book in Chapter 5 for the history of the day and ways to celebrate.

Continue singing the "O Antiphons" for the day. See the "O Antiphons" section of the book for the history and ways to celebrate.

Sing the "O Antiphon" for the day:

"O come, O come, Emmanuel,
and ransom captive Israel,
that mourns in lonely exile here
until the Son of God appear.
Rejoice! Rejoice!
Emmanuel shall come to thee, O Israel!

O come, thou Key of David, come,
and open wide our heavenly home;
make safe the way that leads on high,
and close the path to misery.
Rejoice! Rejoice!
Emmanuel shall come to thee, O Israel!"

The Lord's Prayer

All together
Our Father, who art in heaven,
hallowed be thy Name,
thy kingdom come, thy will be done,
on earth as it is in heaven.

Give us this day our daily bread.
And forgive us our trespasses,
as we forgive those who trespass against us.
And lead us not into temptation,
but deliver us from evil.
For thine is the kingdom,
and the power, and the glory,
for ever and ever. Amen.

The Blessing

Parents lay hands on each of your children and pray this blessing over them:

The Lord bless you and keep you. **Amen.**
The Lord make his face to shine upon you and be gracious to you. **Amen.**
The Lord lift up his countenance upon you and give you peace. **Amen.**

People: **Thanks be to God.**

DECEMBER 21

Start the devotion with the lights lowered or turned off.

Leader: Light and peace, in Jesus Christ our Lord.
People: **Thanks be to God.**
Leader: Let us pray.

If you are using the Great Advent Candle, light it at this time. If you are using an Advent Wreath, light the appropriate candles.

All together
**O gracious light, pure brightness of the everliving
Father in heaven, O Jesus Christ, holy and blessed!
Now as we come to the setting of the sun, and our eyes
behold the vesper light, we sing your praises, O God:
Father, Son, and Holy Spirit.
You are worthy at all times to be praised by happy
voices, O Son of God, O Giver of Life,
and to be glorified through all the worlds.**

A Reading From Holy Scripture

Read: Luke 1:26-38 (ESV)

---

26 In the sixth month the angel Gabriel was sent
from God to a city of Galilee named Nazareth, 27 to
a virgin betrothed to a man whose name was Joseph,
of the house of David. And the virgin's name was

Mary. **28** And he came to her and said, "Greetings, O favored one, the Lord is with you!" **29** But she was greatly troubled at the saying, and tried to discern what sort of greeting this might be. **30** And the angel said to her, "Do not be afraid, Mary, for you have found favor with God. **31** And behold, you will conceive in your womb and bear a son, and you shall call his name Jesus. **32** He will be great and will be called the Son of the Most High. And the Lord God will give to him the throne of his father David, **33** and he will reign over the house of Jacob forever, and of his kingdom there will be no end."

34 And Mary said to the angel, "How will this be, since I am a virgin?"

35 And the angel answered her, "The Holy Spirit will come upon you, and the power of the Most High will overshadow you; therefore the child to be born will be called holy—the Son of God. **36** And behold, your relative Elizabeth in her old age has also conceived a son, and this is the sixth month with her who was called barren. **37** For nothing will be impossible with God." **38** And Mary said, "Behold, I am the servant of the Lord; let it be to me according to your word." And the angel departed from her.

Use this time for other Advent observances: adding hay to the Christmas Crib, hanging a new Jesse Tree ornament, or adding figures to the Nativity Scene.

Continue any Novena (nine days), La Posada or Golden Nights celebrations. See the "La Posada" section of the book in Chapter 5 for the history of the day and ways to celebrate.

Continue singing the "O Antiphons" for the day. See the "O Antiphons" section of the book for the history and ways to celebrate.

Sing the "O Antiphon" for the day"

"O come, O come, Emmanuel,
and ransom captive Israel,
that mourns in lonely exile here
until the Son of God appear.
Rejoice! Rejoice!
Emmanuel shall come to thee, O Israel!

O come, O come, great Lord of might,
who to thy tribes on Sinai's height
in ancient times once gave the law
in cloud, and majesty, and awe.
Rejoice! Rejoice!
Emmanuel shall come to thee, O Israel!"

The Lord's Prayer

All together
Our Father, who art in heaven,
hallowed be thy Name,
thy kingdom come, thy will be done,
on earth as it is in heaven.
Give us this day our daily bread.
And forgive us our trespasses,
as we forgive those who trespass against us.
And lead us not into temptation,
but deliver us from evil.
For thine is the kingdom,
and the power, and the glory,
for ever and ever. Amen.

The Blessing

Parents lay hands on each of your children and pray this blessing over them:

The Lord bless you and keep you. **Amen.**
The Lord make his face to shine upon you and be gracious to you. **Amen.**
The Lord lift up his countenance upon you and give you peace. **Amen.**

People: **Thanks be to God.**

DECEMBER 22

Start the devotion with the lights lowered or turned off.

Leader: Light and peace, in Jesus Christ our Lord.
People: **Thanks be to God.**
Leader: Let us pray.

If you are using the Great Advent Candle, light it at this time. If you are using an Advent Wreath, light the appropriate candles.

All together
**O gracious light, pure brightness of the everliving
Father in heaven, O Jesus Christ, holy and blessed!
Now as we come to the setting of the sun, and our eyes
behold the vesper light, we sing your praises, O God:
Father, Son, and Holy Spirit.
You are worthy at all times to be praised by happy
voices, O Son of God, O Giver of Life,
and to be glorified through all the worlds.**

A Reading From Holy Scripture

Read: Luke 1:39-56 (ESV)

---

39 In those days Mary arose and went with haste into the hill country, to a town in Judah, **40** and she entered the house of Zechariah and greeted Elizabeth. **41** And when Elizabeth heard the greeting of Mary, the baby leaped in her womb. And Elizabeth was filled with the Holy Spirit, 42 and she exclaimed with a loud cry, "Blessed are you among women, and blessed is the fruit of your womb! 43 And why is this granted to me that the mother of my Lord should come to me? 44 For behold, when the sound of your greeting came to my ears, the baby in my womb leaped for joy. 45 And blessed is she who believed that there would be a fulfillment of what was spoken to her from the Lord."

46 And Mary said, "My soul magnifies the Lord, 47 and my spirit rejoices in God my Savior, 48 for he has looked on the humble estate of his servant. For behold, from now on all generations will call me blessed; 49 for he who is mighty has done great things for me, and holy is his name. 50 And his mercy is for those who fear him from generation to generation. 51 He has shown strength with his arm; he has scattered the proud in the thoughts of their hearts; 52 he has brought down the mighty from their thrones and exalted those of humble estate; 53 he has filled the hungry with good things, and the rich he has sent away empty. 54 He has helped his servant Israel, in remembrance of his mercy, 55 as he spoke to our fathers, to Abraham and to his offspring forever."56 And Mary remained with her about three months and returned to her home

Use this time for other Advent observances: adding hay to the Christmas Crib, hanging a new Jesse Tree ornament, or adding figures to the Nativity Scene.

Continue any Novena (nine days), La Posada or Golden Nights celebrations. See the "La Posada" section of the book in Chapter 5 for the history of the day and ways to celebrate.

Continue singing the "O Antiphons" for the day. See the "O Antiphons" section of the book for the history and ways to celebrate.

Sing the "O Antiphon" for the day:

"O come, O come, Emmanuel,
and ransom captive Israel,
that mourns in lonely exile here
until the Son of God appear.
Rejoice! Rejoice!
Emmanuel shall come to thee, O Israel!

O come, thou Root of Jesse's tree,
an ensign of thy people be;
before thee rulers silent fall;
all peoples on thy mercy call.
Rejoice! Rejoice!
Emmanuel shall come to thee, O Israel!"

The Lord's Prayer

All together
Our Father, who art in heaven,
hallowed be thy Name,
thy kingdom come, thy will be done,
on earth as it is in heaven.
Give us this day our daily bread.
And forgive us our trespasses,
as we forgive those who trespass against us.
And lead us not into temptation,
but deliver us from evil.
For thine is the kingdom,
and the power, and the glory,
for ever and ever. Amen.

The Blessing

Parents lay hands on each of your children and pray this blessing over them:

The Lord bless you and keep you. **Amen.**
The Lord make his face to shine upon you and be gracious to you. **Amen.**
The Lord lift up his countenance upon you and give you peace. **Amen.**

People: **Thanks be to God.**

DECEMBER 23

Start the devotion with the lights lowered or turned off.

Leader: Light and peace, in Jesus Christ our Lord.
People: **Thanks be to God.**
Leader: Let us pray.

If you are using the Great Advent Candle, light it at this time. If you are using an Advent Wreath, light the appropriate candles.

All together
**O gracious light, pure brightness of the everliving Father in heaven, O Jesus Christ, holy and blessed! Now as we come to the setting of the sun, and our eyes behold the vesper light, we sing your praises, O God: Father, Son, and Holy Spirit.
You are worthy at all times to be praised by happy voices, O Son of God, O Giver of Life,
and to be glorified through all the worlds.**

A Reading From Holy Scripture

Read: Luke 1:57-80 (ESV)

---

57 Now the time came for Elizabeth to give birth, and she bore a son. **58** And her neighbors and relatives heard that the Lord had shown great mercy to her, and they rejoiced with her. **59** And on the eighth day they came to circumcise the child. And they would have called him Zechariah after his father, **60** but his mother answered, "No; he shall be called John." **61** And they said to her, "None of your relatives is called by this name." **62** And they made signs to his father, inquiring what he wanted him to be called. **63** And he asked for a writing tablet and wrote, "His name is John." And they all wondered. **64** And immediately his mouth was opened and his tongue loosed, and he spoke, blessing God. **65** And fear came on all their neighbors. And all these things were talked about through all the hill country of Judea, **66** and all who heard them laid them up in their hearts, saying, "What then will this child be?" For the hand of the Lord was with him.

67 And his father Zechariah was filled with the Holy Spirit and prophesied, saying,

68 "Blessed be the Lord God of Israel, for he has visited and redeemed his people **69** and has raised up a horn of salvation for us in the house of his servant David, **70** as he spoke by the mouth of his holy prophets from of old, **71** that we should be saved from our enemies and from the hand of all who hate us; **72** to show the mercy promised to our fathers and to remember his holy covenant, **73** the oath that he swore to our father Abraham, to grant us **74** that we, being delivered from the hand of our enemies, might serve him without fear, **75** in holiness and righteousness before him all our days.

76 And you, child, will be called the prophet of the Most High; for you will go before the Lord to prepare his ways, **77** to give knowledge of salvation to his people in the forgiveness of their sins, **78** because of the tender mercy of our God, whereby the sunrise shall visit us from on high **79** to give light to those who sit in darkness and in the shadow of death, to guide our feet into the way of peace."

80 And the child grew and became strong in spirit, and he was in the wilderness until the day of his public appearance to Israel.

Use this time for other Advent observances: adding hay to the Christmas Crib, hanging a new Jesse Tree ornament, or adding figures to the Nativity Scene.

Continue any Novena (nine days), La Posada or Golden Nights celebrations. See the "La Posada" section of the book in Chapter 5 for the history of the day and ways to celebrate.

Continue singing the "O Antiphons" for the day. See the "O Antiphons" section of the book for the history and ways to celebrate.

Sing the "O Antiphon" for the day:

"O come, O come, Emmanuel,
and ransom captive Israel,
that mourns in lonely exile here
until the Son of God appear.
Rejoice! Rejoice!
Emmanuel shall come to thee, O Israel!

O come, Desire of nations, bind
in one the hearts of all mankind;
bid thou our sad divisions cease,
and be thyself our King of Peace.
Rejoice! Rejoice!
Emmanuel shall come to thee, O Israel!"

The Lord's Prayer

All together
Our Father, who art in heaven,
hallowed be thy Name,
thy kingdom come, thy will be done,
on earth as it is in heaven.
Give us this day our daily bread.
And forgive us our trespasses,

as we forgive those who trespass against us.
And lead us not into temptation,
but deliver us from evil.
For thine is the kingdom,
and the power, and the glory,
for ever and ever. Amen.

The Blessing

*Parents lay hands on each of your children and pray this
blessing over them:*

The Lord bless you and keep you. **Amen.**
The Lord make his face to shine upon you and be gracious
to you. **Amen.**
The Lord lift up his countenance upon you and give you
peace. **Amen.**

People: **Thanks be to God.**

DECEMBER 24, CHRISTMAS EVE

Start the devotion with the lights lowered or off. The patriarch, prophet, Mary and John the Baptist candles should already be lit.

Leader: Light and peace, in Jesus Christ our Lord.
People: **Thanks be to God.**
Leader: Let us pray.

Leader:

Lord Jesus Christ, on this day we celebrate your birth at Bethlehem and we are drawn to kneel in wonder at heaven touching earth: accept our heartfelt praise as we worship you, our Savior and our eternal God. **Amen.**

If you are using the Great Advent Candle, light it at this time. If you are using an Advent Wreath, the Jesus Candle (the white candle in the middle) is lit at this time.

All together
O gracious light, pure brightness of the everliving Father in heaven, O Jesus Christ, holy and blessed! Now as we come to the setting of the sun, and our eyes behold the vesper light, we sing your praises, O God: Father, Son, and Holy Spirit. You are worthy at all times to be praised by happy voices, O Son of God, O Giver of Life, and to be glorified through all the worlds.

A Reading From Holy Scripture

Read: Luke 2:1-20 (ESV)

---

1 In those days a decree went out from Caesar Augustus that all the world should be registered. **2** This was the first registration when Quirinius was governor of Syria. **3** And all went to be registered, each to his own town. **4** And Joseph also went up from Galilee, from the town of Nazareth, to Judea, to the city of David, which is called Bethlehem, because he was of the house and lineage of David, **5** to be registered with Mary, his betrothed, who was with child. **6** And while they were there, the time came for her to give birth. **7** And she gave birth to her firstborn son and wrapped him in swaddling cloths and laid him in a manger, because there was no place for them in the inn.

8 And in the same region there were shepherds out in the field, keeping watch over their flock by night. **9** And an angel of the Lord appeared to them, and the glory of the Lord shone around them, and they were filled with great fear. **10** And the angel said to them, "Fear not, for behold, I bring you good news of great joy that will be for all the people. **11** For unto you is born this day in the city of David a Savior, who is Christ the Lord. **12** And this will be a sign for you: you will find a baby wrapped in swaddling cloths and lying in a manger." **13** And suddenly there was with the angel a multitude of the heavenly host praising God and saying, 14 "Glory to God in the highest, and on earth peace among those with whom he is pleased!"

15 When the angels went away from them into heaven, the shepherds said to one another, "Let us go over to Bethlehem and see this thing that has happened, which the Lord has made known to us." 16 And they went with haste and found Mary and Joseph, and the baby lying in a manger. 17 And when they saw it, they made known the saying that had been told them concerning this child. 18 And all who heard it wondered at what the shepherds told them. 19 But Mary treasured up all these things, pondering them in her heart. 20 And the shepherds returned, glorifying and praising God for all they had heard and seen, as it had been told them.

Use this time for other Advent observances: adding hay to the Christmas Crib, hanging a new Jesse Tree ornament, or adding figures to the Nativity Scene.

The Lord's Prayer

All together
**Our Father, who art in heaven,
hallowed be thy Name,
thy kingdom come, thy will be done,
on earth as it is in heaven.
Give us this day our daily bread.
And forgive us our trespasses,
as we forgive those who trespass against us.
And lead us not into temptation,
but deliver us from evil.
For thine is the kingdom,
and the power, and the glory,
for ever and ever. Amen.**

The Blessing

Parents lay hands on each of your children and pray this blessing over them:

The Lord bless you and keep you. **Amen.**
The Lord make his face to shine upon you and be gracious to you. **Amen.**
The Lord lift up his countenance upon you and give you peace. **Amen.**

People: **Thanks be to God.**

DECEMBER 25, CHRISTMAS DAY

Start the devotion with the lights lowered or off. All of the Advent candles should already be lit.

Leader: Light and peace, in Jesus Christ our Lord.
People: **Thanks be to God.**
Leader: Let us pray.

Opening prayer:

Lord Jesus Christ, on this day we celebrate your birth at Bethlehem and we are drawn to kneel in wonder at heaven touching earth: accept our heartfelt praise as we worship you, our Savior and our eternal God. **Amen.**

All together
**O gracious light, pure brightness of the everliving
Father in heaven, O Jesus Christ, holy and blessed!
Now as we come to the setting of the sun, and our eyes
behold the vesper light, we sing your praises, O God:
Father, Son, and Holy Spirit.
You are worthy at all times to be praised by happy
voices, O Son of God, O Giver of Life,
and to be glorified through all the worlds.**

A Reading From Holy Scripture

Read: John 1:1-14 (ESV)

---

1 In the beginning was the Word, and the Word was with God, and the Word was God. 2 He was in the beginning with God. 3 All things were made through him, and without him was not any thing made that was made. 4 In him was life, and the life was the light of men. 5 The light shines in the darkness, and the darkness has not overcome it.

6 There was a man sent from God, whose name was John. 7 He came as a witness, to bear witness about the light, that all might believe through him. 8 He was not the light, but came to bear witness about the light. 9 The true light, which gives light to everyone, was coming into the world. 10 He was in the world, and the world was made through him, yet the world did not know him. 11 He came to his own, and his own people did not receive him. 12 But to all who did receive him, who believed in his name, he gave the right to become children of God, 13 who were born, not of blood nor of the will of the flesh nor of the will of man, but of God.

14 And the Word became flesh and dwelt among us, and we have seen his glory, glory as of the only Son from the Father, full of grace and truth.

The Lord's Prayer

All together
**Our Father, who art in heaven,
hallowed be thy Name,
thy kingdom come, thy will be done,
on earth as it is in heaven.
Give us this day our daily bread.
And forgive us our trespasses,
as we forgive those who trespass against us.
And lead us not into temptation,
but deliver us from evil.
For thine is the kingdom,
and the power, and the glory,
for ever and ever. Amen.**

The Blessing

Parents lay hands on each of your children and pray this blessing over them:

The Lord bless you and keep you. **Amen.**
The Lord make his face to shine upon you and be gracious to you. **Amen.**
The Lord lift up his countenance upon you and give you peace. **Amen.**

People: **Thanks be to God.**

THE SUNDAYS OF ADVENT

There are many traditions surrounding the Sundays of Advent. For some the Advent Candles symbolize Hope, Peace, Joy, and Love. In this book, we follow the Anglican tradition that looks to the saints and prophets who have come before us. These prayers may be used as you light the candles on each Sunday in Advent.

The First Sunday of Advent

Leader:

God and Father of Abraham and Sarah, and all the patriarchs and matriarchs of old, you are our Father, too. Your love is revealed to us in Jesus Christ, Son of God and Son of David. Help us in preparing to celebrate his birth to make our hearts ready for your Holy Spirit to make his home among us. We ask this through Jesus Christ, the light who is coming into the world. Amen.

If you are using the Great Advent Candle, light it at this time. If you are using an Advent Wreath, the Patriarch Candle (the first violet or blue candle) is lit at this time.

The Second Sunday of Advent

Leader:

God our Father, you spoke to the prophets of old of a Savior who would bring peace. You helped them to spread the joyful message of his coming kingdom. Help us, as we prepare to celebrate his birth, to share with those around us the good news of your power and love. We ask this through Jesus Christ, the light who is coming into the world. Amen.

If you are using the Great Advent Candle, light it at this time. If you are using an Advent Wreath, the Prophet Candle (the second violet or blue candle) is lit at this time.

The Third Sunday of Advent

Leader:

God our Father, the angel Gabriel told the Virgin Mary that she was to be the mother of your Son. Though Mary was afraid, she responded to your call with joy. Help us, whom you call to serve you, to share like her in your great work of bringing to our world your love and healing. We ask this through Jesus Christ, the light who is coming into the world. Amen.

If you are using the Great Advent Candle, light it at this time. If you are using an Advent Wreath, the Mary Candle (the pink candle) is lit at this time.

The Fourth Sunday of Advent

Leader:

God our Father, you gave to Zechariah and Elizabeth in their old age a son called John. He grew up strong in spirit, prepared the people for the coming of the Lord, and baptized them in the Jordan to wash away their sins. Help us, who have been baptized into Christ, to be ready to welcome him into our hearts, and to grow strong in faith by the power of the Spirit. We ask this through Jesus Christ, the light who is coming into the world. Amen.

If you are using the Great Advent Candle, light it at this time. If you are using an Advent Wreath, the John the Baptist Candle (the third purple or blue candle) is lit at this time.

ADVENT RECIPES

*T*raditional Advent and Christmas recipes from around the world.

BISSCHOPSWIJN OR BISHOP'S WINE

Made for the Eve of the Feast of St. Nicholas.

> 2 bottles full -bodied red wine
> 1 orange, studded with cloves and
>   quartered
> 1 strip lemon peel
> 1 stick of cinnamon
> 1/4 teaspoon each: mace, allspice,
>   ground ginger
> 2 to 4 tablespoons sugar to taste

Pour the wine into a saucepan. Add the orange, lemon peel, stick of cinnamon and spices. Simmer for 5 to 10 minutes. Add sugar to taste. Serve hot.

Recipe from Maria Von Trapp

BUCHE DE NOEL OR CHRISTMAS LOG

Made on Christmas Eve or Christmas Day.

Sponge Cake:
4 eggs, separated and at room
    temperature
1 cup sugar
1/4 cup hot water
Grated rind of 1 lemon
1 teaspoon lemon juice
1/2 teaspoon vanilla
1 cup sifted flour
1 teaspoon baking powder
1/4 teaspoon salt
A few tablespoons rum (optional)
confectioner's sugar

Preheat oven to 400 degrees. Grease a jelly-roll pan, 10 by 15 inches. Line the pan with waxed paper and grease the paper.

Beat the yolks until light and lemon colored. Gradually add the sugar, beating until very thick. Beat in the hot water, lemon rind, juice and vanilla.

Sift the flour with the baking powder and salt, and gradually beat into the egg mixture. Whip the egg whites until stiff but not dry. Fold gently but thoroughly into the batter.

Pour it into the jelly roll pan. Bake 12 to 15 minutes, or until the cake is lightly browned.

As soon as the cake is done, sprinkle it with the rum if you wish. Spread a clean, damp kitchen towel on the counter. Cover it with waxed paper. Sprinkle the paper with confectioners sugar. Invert the cake onto the waxed paper. Peel the paper off of the cake and trim the cake if too crusty. Roll up the cake along the long side with the towel and waxed paper. Let it cool to room temperature.

> Mocha Cream Icing:
> 4 egg yolks
> 1 1/4 cups sugar
> 1/3 cup water
> 2 teaspoons vanilla extract
> 2 teaspoons instant coffee
> 2 ounces unsweetened chocolate,
>   melted and cooled
> 3 sticks butter, at room temperature

Beat the yolks until light-colored and thick. Combine the sugar and water in a saucepan. Cook to the soft-ball stage: about 234 degrees on a candy thermometer. Beating constantly, add the eggs to the syrup. Continue beating until mixture is cool. Stir in the vanilla extract, coffee and chocolate. Gradually beat in the butter. Cool the icing in the refrigerator if it is too soft.

Unroll the cake. Spread it with half of the icing. Without the paper and the towel, roll it up as tightly as possible without damaging it. Chill for several hours. Chill the icing as well. Trim the ends of the cake on the diagonal; reserve the scraps. Frost the cake with most of the remaining icing. Cut the scraps to resemble knot holes. Set them on the main log and ice them. Using the tines of a fork, make marks on the surface of the cake to look like bark.

Recipe from *A Continual Feast*

BUNUELOS (MEXICAN FRITTERS)

Made on Christmas Eve or Christmas Day.

Fritters:

    3 cups flour
    1 tablespoon sugar
    2 teaspoons baking powder
    1/2 teaspoon salt
    3/4 cup milk
    1 egg
    2 tablespoons lard, melted and cooled
    2 teaspoons vanilla
    Vegetable oil, for frying

Cinnamon Sugar:

    1 cup sugar
    1 tablespoon cinnamon

Anise Syrup (optional):

    2 cups water
    8 ounces Mexican brown sugar,
       coarsely chopped
    1 teaspoon grated lime peel
    1 teaspoon grated orange peel
    2 cinnamon sticks
    2 teaspoons anise seed

For the fritters:

Mix flour, sugar, baking powder and salt in medium bowl. Set aside. Mix milk, egg, lard and vanilla in large bowl until well blended. Gradually add flour mixture, stirring constantly to form a slightly sticky dough. Turn dough out onto lightly floured surface. Incorporate additional flour, a tablespoon flour at a time, until dough is no longer sticky. Divide dough into 16 equal pieces. Shape each into a ball. Place in bowl. Cover with plastic wrap. Let dough rest 30 minutes.

For the cinnamon sugar:

Mix sugar and cinnamon in medium bowl. Set aside. For the Anise Syrup, mix water, Mexican brown sugar, lime peel, orange peel, cinnamon sticks and anise seed in heavy-bottomed 3-quart saucepan. Cook on medium heat 5 minutes, stirring to dissolve Mexican brown sugar. Bring to boil on medium-high heat. Boil 20 minutes or until syrup thinly coats a spoon. Strain and set aside at room temperature. (Anise Syrup can be made 3 to 4 days ahead. Cover and refrigerate. Rewarm before using.)

Roll each ball of dough into a 6-inch round on lightly floured surface. Stack dough rounds between wax paper or plastic wrap. Let stand 10 minutes.

Pour vegetable oil into heavy large skillet or saucepan to depth of 1 inch (about 2 cups oil). Heat oil on medium-high heat to 365°F to 370°F on deep-fry thermometer. Fry dough rounds, 1 at a time, for 2 minutes or until golden and puffed, turning once using tongs. Drain on paper towels. Sprinkle each fritter with 1 tablespoon cinnamon sugar mixture. Serve with warm Anise Syrup, if desired.

Recipe from McCormick.com

CHRISTMAS PUNCH

Made on Christmas Eve or Christmas Day.

1 sliced pineapple
1 lb. sugar
1 bottle claret
1 bottle of red wine
1/2 bottle rum
juice of 4 lemons
juice of 4 oranges
1 pint water
grated rind of 1 lemon
grated rind of 1 orange
4 whole oranges cut in pieces
1 stick cinnamon, broken up
1 vanilla bean
1/2 cup maraschino cherries
1 bottle champagne

Boil spices thoroughly with the water. Remove them and pour the water into large earthenware pot. Add lemon and orange and rind, as well as pineapple and sugar (fruit and sugar prepared in a separate dish). Then add wine and rum, cover and heat. Add champagne before serving. (This is only for adults! Make Christmas Punch for Children for the kids).

Recipe from Maria Von Trapp

CHRISTMAS PUNCH FOR CHILDREN

Made on Christmas Eve or Christmas Day.

> 1 quart grape juice
> 2 quarts water
> 2 cups sugar
> 1/2 teaspoon whole cloves
> 1 stick cinnamon
> juice of 2 lemons
> juice of 2 oranges
> rind of 2 lemons
> rind of 2 oranges

Boil sugar, water, lemon rind, and spices until flavored. Mix with the rest of the ingredients, boil five minutes, and serve hot in punch glasses.

Recipe from Maria Von Trapp

CRISTOLLEN

Made on the baking days before Christmas.

    4 3/4 to 5 1/4 cups all-purpose flour
    2 packages active dry yeast
    1 teaspoon ground cardamom
    1 1/4 cups milk
    1/2 cup sugar
    1/2 cup butter
    3/4 teaspoon salt
    1 egg
    1 cup diced mixed candied fruits and
        peels
    1 cup raisins
    3/4 cup chopped walnuts
    1 tablespoon finely shredded
        lemon peel

In a large mixing bowl stir together 2 cups of flour, yeast, and cardamom. In a medium saucepan heat and stir the milk, sugar, butter, and salt until warm (120-130 degrees) and butter is almost melted. Add to flour mixture along with egg. Beat with an electric mixer on low speed for 30 seconds, scraping bowl constantly. Beat on high speed for 3 minutes. Using a spoon, stir in candied fruits and peels, raisins, walnuts, and lemon peel; stir in as much of the remaining flour as you can.

Turn out onto a lightly floured surface. Knead in enough remaining flour to make a moderately soft dough that is smooth and elastic (3 to 5 minutes total). Shape into a ball. Place in a greased bowl; turn once to grease surface. Cover and let rise in a warm place until double (about 1 to 1 1/2 hours).

Punch dough down. Turn out onto a lightly floured surface. Divide dough in half; divide each half into thirds. Cover and let rest for 10 minutes. Meanwhile, grease 2 baking sheets.

With hands, roll each piece of dough into a 1-inch-thick rope about 15 inches long. Line up 3 of the ropes, 1 inch apart, on prepared baking sheet. Starting in the middle, loosely braid by bringing the left rope under the center rope. Repeat to end of loaf. On the other end, braid by bringing alternate ropes over center rope from center. Press rope ends on each side together to seal. Repeat braiding with the remaining 3 ropes on other prepared baking sheet. Cover and let rise until nearly double (about 1 hour).

Brush loaves with milk. Bake in a 350 degree oven for 20 to 25 minutes or until golden and loaves sound hollow when tapped. (Switch baking sheets to a different oven rack halfway through baking time to ensure even baking.) If necessary, cover with foil the last few minutes to prevent over browning. Remove from baking sheets. Cool on wire racks.

Recipe from *A Continual Feast*

CUCCIA

Made on the Feast of St. Lucia.

> 1 cup dried wheat berries
> 1/4 teaspoon salt
> 1 1/2 cups whole-milk ricotta
> 2 tablespoons granulated sugar
> 1/8 teaspoon vanilla extract
> Ground cinnamon, for garnish
> Dark chocolate, either miniature
>   chips or shaved with a vegetable
>   peeler or microplane, for garnish

Place wheat berries in a medium saucepan, cover with water by 2 to 3 inches, and season with kosher salt. Bring to a boil over high heat and then reduce to a simmer, cooking uncovered until wheat berries are tender, about 50 to 60 minutes. Using a fine mesh strainer, drain berries and run under cool water until chilled. Place strainer of berries over a large bowl and let drain for at least 15 minutes.

While wheat berries cook, combine ricotta, sugar, and vanilla in a mixing bowl. Using a whisk or immersion blender, whip until creamy and smooth.

Fold cooled wheat berries into ricotta mixture. Cuccia may be served immediately or stored in the fridge in a tightly sealed container for up to 1 week. To serve, spoon into individual bowls, dust with a pinch of cinnamon, and top with shaved chocolate or chocolate chips to taste.

Recipe from www.seriouseats.com

EGGNOG

Made on Christmas Eve and Christmas Day.

> 4 egg yolks
> 1/3 cup sugar, plus 1 tablespoon
> 1 pint whole milk
> 1 cup heavy cream
> 3 ounces bourbon
> 1 teaspoon freshly grated nutmeg
> 4 egg whites*

In the bowl of a stand mixer, beat the egg yolks until they lighten in color. Gradually add the 1/3 cup sugar and continue to beat until it is completely dissolved. Add the milk, cream, bourbon and nutmeg and stir to combine.

Place the egg whites in the bowl of a stand mixer and beat to soft peaks. With mixer still running gradually add 1 tablespoon of sugar and beat until stiff peaks form. Whisk the egg whites into the mixture. Chill and serve.

Cook's Note: For cooked eggnog, follow the procedure below.

In the bowl of a stand mixer, beat the egg yolks until they lighten in color. Gradually add 1/3 cup sugar and continue to beat until it is completely dissolved. Set aside.

In a medium saucepan, over high heat, combine milk, heavy cream and nutmeg and bring just to a boil, stirring occasionally. Remove from the heat and gradually temper the hot mixture into the egg and sugar mixture. Then return everything to the pot and cook until mixture reaches 160 degrees F. Remove from the heat, stir in bourbon, pour into a medium mixing bowl, and set in the refrigerator to chill.

In a medium mixing bowl, beat the egg whites to soft peaks. With the mixer running gradually add 1 tablespoon of sugar and beat until stiff peaks form. Whisk the egg whites into the chilled mixture.

Recipe from foodnetwork.com

FRENCH HOT CHOCOLATE

Made on Christmas Eve and Christmas Day.

2 ounces dark chocolate per cup of
whole milk

Heat the milk in a saucepan at a medium heat. Break the chocolate into small pieces and add to the milk. Stir until the chocolate is melted and serve.

KERALA FRUIT CAKE FROM INDIA

Made on Christmas Eve and Christmas Day.

> 1 cup plain flour
> ½ cup chopped cashew nuts
> ¼ cup black raisins
> ½ cup mixed dry fruits (dates,
>   cherries, orange peels, etc)
> ½ cup sugar (for sugar syrup)
> ¾ cup sugar (for cake batter)
> ⅔ cup unsalted butter, at room
>   temperature
> 3 eggs
> ½ teaspoon cinnamon powder
> ¼ teaspoon clove powder (see notes)
> 1 teaspoon of baking powder
> 1 teaspoon vanilla extract
> A pinch of salt

In a pan on medium heat, melt ½ cup sugar slowly. It will first melt and then turn into a dark brown goop. Keep stirring and let it turn a deep dark caramel color. Don't let it burn. Turn off heat and add about ¼ cup water. The sugar will harden. Turn the heat back on and slowly heat the mixture until the sugar crystals dissolve. This will take around 10 mins. Let this cool and set aside.

Preheat oven to 350 degrees. Add 3 tablespoons flour to the dry fruits and nuts and dredge completely to coat it. Set aside.

Mix the remaining flour and baking powder, spices, and salt until well combined.

Beat the butter and ¾ cup sugar until fluffy, about 10 mins by hand, 3-4 mins with an electric beater. Add vanilla and mix until combined. Next, add 1 egg and beat. Then add a bit of the flour mixture and fold. Likewise, alternate between the eggs and flour mixture until they are used up.

Add the cooled caramel and dredged fruits and gently fold in. Pour batter into a greased cake pan and smooth the top.

Bake for 50-55 minutes until the top turns a dark brown and when a skewer inserted into the cake comes out with dry crumbs. Start checking from 45 mins to see if the cake is done. The top will look like it's overdone but don't worry, make sure the inside is also completely cooked.

Dust with icing sugar when the cake is completely cooled

Recipe from cookingandme.com

KHEER (INDIAN RICE PUDDING)

¼ cup long grain rice or Basmati rice
2 ½ cups milk
¼ cup sugar
¼ teaspoon green cardamom seeds
   powder
few strands saffron
½ tablespoon almonds
½ tablespoon cashew nuts
½ tablespoon raisins

Wash the rice under running cold water till water runs clear. Soak them in enough water for 20-30 minutes. While rice is soaking, chop the nuts and set aside. After soaking time, discard the water.

Take milk in a heavy bottom pan. Turn the heat on medium. Let the milk come to a boil. Once it starts boiling, add rice. Stir well and let it simmer on low-medium heat 20-25 minutes. Or till the rice is tender and cooked. Do stir every five minutes and make sure that rice or milk is not sticking to the pan. Check by pinching the rice grain, it will mash very easily. When you take a spoonful of it and pour it back, rice and milk stay separate. Add sugar and cardamom powder. Stir it well. Add saffron strands and chopped cashews, almonds and raisins. Mix well. let it simmer for 6-7 minutes. It should be thick now.

How to check right consistency: take a ladleful of kheer and pour it back. rice and milk should fall together in the same flow. They should not be separated like earlier.

Recipe from cookingandme.com

KLETZENBROT (BREAD WITH DRIED FRUIT)

Made on the Feast of St. Thomas.

> 2 cups whole wheat flour
> 1 cup white flour
> 2/3 cup brown sugar
> 3 teaspoons baking powder
> 2 teaspoon baking soda
> 1/4 teaspoon salt
> 2 cups buttermilk
> 1 cup chopped nuts
> 1 cup chopped prunes
> 1 cup chopped figs
> 1 cup chopped dates
> 1/2 cup raisins
> 1/2 cup currants

Mix sifted dry ingredients in a bowl. Add buttermilk slowly and stir to a smooth dough. Mix in the nuts, raisins, and the rest. Bake at 350 degrees for about an hour.

Recipe from *A Continual Feast*

LEBKUCHEN (A GERMAN HONEY CAKE)

Made on the Feast of St. Nicolas and on the baking days before Christmas

> 1 1/3 cups honey
> 1/3 cup packed brown sugar
> 2 cups all-purpose flour
> 1 teaspoon baking powder
> 1/2 teaspoon baking soda
> 1 cup candied mixed fruit
> 1 tablespoon light sesame oil
> 1/4 teaspoon ground ginger
> 1/2 teaspoon ground cardamom
> 2 teaspoons ground cinnamon
> 1/4 teaspoon ground cloves
> 1/4 teaspoon ground allspice
>   (optional)
> 1/4 teaspoon ground nutmeg
>   (optional)
> 1 1/2 cups all-purpose flour

Spray the bottom and sides of a 10 x 15 inch glass pan with a non-stick spray. Preheat oven to 325 degrees.

In a 2 cup glass measuring cup, heat the honey and 1/3 cup sugar in a microwave for 1 minute. Pour this mixture into a medium mixing bowl. Sift together flour, baking powder, and baking soda. Add to the honey mixture. Stir well.

Add and mix in by hand the candied fruit, oil, and spices. Add 1 1/2 to 2 cups more flour. Knead dough to mix (dough will be stiff). Spread into pan. Bake for 20 minutes until inserted toothpick comes out clean.

Cut into squares. May be frosted with sugar glaze or eaten plain. Best if stored for 2 weeks.

Recipe from *A Continual Feast*

MULLED CIDER

Made on Christmas Eve and Christmas Day.

> 2 quarts cider or apple juice
> Peel of one orange or 2 teaspoons
>   orange extract
> 1 to 2 sticks of cinnamon
> 1/2 tsp. allspice
> 1/2 tsp. cloves

Put all ingredients in a saucepan and bring to a boil. Lower the heat and simmer 5 to 10 minutes.

PANETTONE (ITALIAN CHRISTMAS BREAD)

Made on Christmas Eve and Christmas Day.

Marinated fruit:

> 1/3 cup golden raisins
> 1/3 cup chopped dried apricots
> 1/3 cup dried tart cherries
> 1/4 cup triple sec (orange-flavored
>   liqueur) or orange juice

Dough:

> 1 package dry yeast (about 2 1/4
>   teaspoons)
> 1/4 teaspoon granulated sugar
> 1/4 cup warm water (100° to 110°)
> 3 3/4 cups all-purpose flour, divided
> 6 tablespoons butter or stick
>   margarine, melted
> 1/4 cup whole milk
> 1/4 cup granulated sugar
> 1/2 teaspoon salt
> 1 large egg
> 1 large egg yolk
> 2 tablespoons pine nuts
> Cooking spray
> 1 teaspoon butter, melted
> 2 teaspoons sugar

To prepare marinated fruit, combine first 4 ingredients in a small bowl; let stand 1 hour. Drain fruit in a sieve over a bowl, reserving fruit and 2 teaspoons liqueur separately.

To prepare dough, dissolve yeast and 1/4 teaspoon granulated sugar in warm water in a small bowl; let stand 5 minutes. Lightly spoon flour into dry measuring cups; level with a knife. Combine 1/2 cup flour and next 6 ingredients (1/2 cup flour through egg yolk) in a large bowl; beat at medium speed of a mixer 1 minute or until smooth. Add yeast mixture and 1/2 cup flour; beat 1 minute. Stir in marinated fruit, 2 1/2 cups flour, and pine nuts.

Turn dough out onto a lightly floured surface. Knead until smooth and elastic (about 8 minutes); add enough of remaining flour, 1 tablespoon at a time, to prevent dough from sticking to hands. Place dough in a large bowl coated with cooking spray, turning to coat top. Cover and let rise in a warm place (85°), free from drafts, about 1 1/2 hours. Dough will not double in size. (Press two fingers into dough. If indentation remains, the dough has risen enough.) Punch dough down; let rest 5 minutes.

Divide in half, shaping each into a ball. Place balls into 2 (13-ounce) coffee cans coated with cooking spray. Cover and let rise 1 hour.

Preheat oven to 375°. Uncover dough. Place coffee cans on bottom rack in oven, and bake at 375° for 30 minutes or until browned and loaf sounds hollow when tapped. Remove bread from cans, and cool on a wire rack. Combine reserved 2 teaspoons liqueur and 1 teaspoon butter; brush over loaves. Sprinkle evenly with sugar.

Recipe from myrecipes.com

PONCHE (MEXICAN CHRISTMAS PUNCH)

Made on Christmas Eve and Christmas Day.

> 4 quarts water
> 2 cinnamon sticks
> 8 whole cloves
> 5 long tamarind pods, husk removed,
>   and seeded or boil the entire pod
>   to make removing easier
> ½ pound tejocotes or crab apples, left
>   whole
> 6 large guavas, peeled and cut into
>   large bite-size chunks
> 2 red apples (of your choice), peeled,
>   cored, and cut into small bite-size
>   chunks
> 1 pear (of your choice), peeled, cored,
>   and cut into small bite-size chunks
> 2 (4-inch) sugarcane sticks, peeled
>   and cut into small chunks
> 1 cup pitted prunes
> 1/2 cup dark raisins
> 1 orange, sliced
> 1 cone piloncillo, chopped or 1 cup
>   dark brown sugar
> 1 ounce brandy or tequila per cup
>   (optional)

In a large pot, over high heat, boil water, cinnamon sticks, cloves, tamarind, and tejocotes. After it starts to boil, lower the heat and simmer for about 10 minutes until the tejocotes are soft. Remove the tejocotes from the heat, peel, remove hard ends, cut in half, and deseed. Return them to the pot. Add guavas, apples, pears, sugar cane, prunes, orange slices, and piloncillo. Simmer for at least 30 minutes, stirring gently. Discard cinnamon sticks and cloves. Ladle into cups, making sure each cup gets some chunks of fruit. Add brandy or tequila to each cup (optional).

Recipe from muybuenocooking.com

PLUM PUDDING

Made on the last Sunday before Advent which is known as "Stir-Up Sunday" or the First Sunday in Advent and served on Christmas Day

> ⅔ cup each:
> currants
> dark raisins
> golden raisins
> dates or prunes, chopped
> ¾ cup chopped candied orange or
>   lemon peel
> ½ cup brandy, rum, sherry or cider
> 1 cup fine breadcrumbs
> 1 teaspoon cinnamon

½ teaspoon ground ginger
¼ teaspoon nutmeg
¼ teaspoon ground cloves
1 teaspoon salt
1 ½ cups dark or light brown sugar
1 ½ cups stout, ale, beer or milk
4 eggs, well beaten
⅔ cup beef suet, finely chopped
¾ cup flour
1 ½ teaspoons baking powder
½ teaspoon baking soda
Freshly grated rind of one lemon
Freshly grated rind of one orange
½ cup finely chopped blanched
   almonds
⅔ cup peeled, cored, chopped apples

Combine the dried and candied fruits. Pour the brandy over them and let them sit for at least 1 hour. Mix the crumbs with the spices, salt and brown sugar. Pour the stout over them and let stand for a few minutes. Blend the eggs with the suet. Sift the flour with the baking powder and baking soda. Combine all these mixtures and add the remaining ingredients: the rinds, the almonds and the apples. Turn this mixture into a well-buttered and sugared 2-quart mold. Cover well with aluminum foil. Place the mold on a rack in a large pan. Pour in 2 to 3 inches of water. Cover the pot well. Steam for about three hours, or until the pudding is firm. (A knife inserted into the middle of the pudding should come out clean. You will need to unwrap the pudding to check and then re-wrap.) Store in the refrigerator; to re-heat, steam for an hour or so.

Recipe from *A Continual Feast*

SAFFRON BUNS

Made on the Feast of St. Lucia.

> 3/4 cup milk
> 1/2 teaspoon saffron threads
> 1 teaspoon plus 1/4 cup granulated
>   sugar
> 1 1/4-ounce packet active dry yeast
> 3 1/2 to 4 cups all purpose flour
> 1/2 teaspoon salt
> The seeds from 3 cardamom pods,
>   ground (optional)
> 1/4 cup unsalted butter, softened
> 1/4 cup of sour cream
> 2 large eggs
> Raisins

Glaze

> 1 egg, beaten

In a small pot, heat the milk, saffron, and 1 teaspoon of sugar together until the milk is steamy. Remove from heat and stir to dissolve the sugar. Let cool until about 115 degrees, or warm to the touch but not hot.

Sprinkle the yeast over the warm saffron-infused milk and let sit for 5 to 10 minutes until foamy.

In a mixer, whisk together 3 1/2 cups of the flour, remaining 1/4 cup of sugar, salt and ground cardamom (if using).

Make a well in the center of the flour and add the yeast milk saffron mixture, the eggs, the butter, and the sour cream. Mix the ingredients until well incorporated.

Switch to the dough hook of your mixer (if using, otherwise knead by hand). On low speed start to knead the dough. Slowly add additional flour, a tablespoon at a time, kneading to incorporate after each addition. Do this until the dough is still a little sticky to the touch, but does not completely stick to your hands when you handle it.

Shape the dough into a ball and place in a large bowl. Cover with plastic wrap. (Note at this point you can make ahead and refrigerate overnight if you wish.)

Let sit in a warm place for 1 to 2 hours, until the dough has doubled in size. (One way to tell that the dough is ready is that you poke your finger in it and it takes quite a bit of time for the indentation left by your finger to go away.)

When the dough has doubled in size, gently press it down and knead it a couple of times. Break off a piece and form it into a ball about 2 inches wide. Roll the ball out into a snake, about 14 inches long. Then curl the ends in opposite directions, forming an "S" with spirals at each end. Place on a lined baking sheet and repeat with the rest of the dough.

Cover with plastic wrap and place in a warm spot until the dough shapes double in size, 30 minutes to an hour.

Preheat oven to 400 degrees. Using a pastry brush, brush some beaten egg over the tops and sides of the uncooked buns. Place raisins in the centers of the "S" spirals.

Place in the oven and bake at 400°F for about 10 to 11 minutes (turning halfway through cooking to ensure even browning), until the buns are golden brown. Remove from oven and let cool for 5 minutes before eating.

Recipe from www.simplyrecipes.com

SAINT LUCY'S CROWN

Made on St. Lucy's Day.

    1/4 - 1/2 teaspoon saffron threads
    1 cup lukewarm milk
    2 packages dry yeast
    1/4 cup of warm water (100-110
        degrees F)
    1/2 cup sugar
    1 teaspoon salt
    1/3 cup sweet butter
    1 egg, lightly beaten
    4 cups flour
    Grated rind of 1 lemon
    4-5 tablespoons blanched almonds,
        grated or finely chopped
    4-5 tablespoons chopped candied
        citron (optional)
    Confectioners' Sugar Glaze (see
        recipe below)
    Tapers or thin candles (optional)

Crush the saffron to a fine powder, and steep it in a tablespoon or two of the lukewarm milk for about 10 minutes. In a large bowl, dissolve the yeast in the lukewarm water. Stir in 1 tablespoon of the sugar. Set the mixture aside for 5 to 10 minutes, or until frothy.

Scald the remaining milk. Stir in the rest of the sugar, and the salt and butter. Stir until the butter is melted. Let cool to lukewarm. Stir into the yeast mixture. Add the saffron milk and lightly beaten egg. Stir in the flour gradually, mixing well. Add the lemon rind, almonds, and citron.

Turn the dough out onto a lightly floured surface. Knead for about 10 minutes, or until the dough is smooth and elastic. While you are kneading, add more flour if the dough is sticky.

Place the dough in a greased bowl, turning to grease the top. Cover and let rise in a draft-free spot until doubled in bulk, about 1 to 1 1/2 hours.

Punch the dough down. Cut off one-third to make the top braid; set aside. Divide the remaining dough into three parts. Roll each part into a rope about 25 inches long. Place the three ropes close together on a buttered baking sheet and braid them together. (Try starting from the middle; you may find it easier.) Form the braid into a circle, pinching the ends to seal.

Divide the reserved dough into three parts. Roll each part into a rope about 24 inches long. Proceed as above: Place the three ropes close together on a buttered baking sheet and braid them together. Form the braid into a circle, pinching the ends to seal.

Cover both braids lightly and let the bread rise for 30-45 minutes, or until almost doubled in bulk.

Bake at 400 degrees for 10 minutes. Reduce the heat to 350 degrees and bake for about 40 minutes longer, or until the two braided rings are golden brown and sound hollow when tapped on the bottom.

Place the smaller braid on top of the larger. Drizzle over it the Confectioners' Sugar Glaze. Optional: Stick thin tapers into the crown and light them. There is no fixed number of tapers; why not put in one for each member of your family?

Variations:

You can eliminate the saffron and flavor the crown with 2 teaspoons ground cardamom; add it along with the salt.

Confectioners' Sugar Glaze

    2-3 teaspoons lemon juice or milk or
      water
    1/2-1 cup confectioner's sugar

Stir the lemon juice into the confectioners' sugar; mix well. Add more sugar or lemon juice as needed to produce a proper consistency for drizzling.

Recipe from *A Continual Feast*

SPECULATIUS

Made for the Eve and the Feast of St. Nicholas and the baking days for Christmas.

1 cup butter
1 cup shortening
2 cups brown sugar
1/2 cup sour cream
1/2 teaspoon soda
4 teaspoons cinnamon
1/2 teaspoon nutmeg
1/2 teaspoon cloves
4 1/2 cups sifted flour
1/2 cup chopped nuts

Cream the butter, shortening and sugar. Add sour cream alternately with sifted dry ingredients. Stir in nuts. Knead the dough and shape into rolls. Wrap the rolls in plastic wrap and chill overnight. Roll the dough very thin and cut into shapes. Bake at 350 degrees for 10 to 15 minutes.

Recipe from *A Continual Feast*

SUGAR COOKIES

Made on the baking days before Christmas.

> 1 cup butter
> 1 1/2 cups sifted confectioner's sugar
> 1 egg
> 1 teaspoon vanilla
> 1/2 teaspoon almond
> 2 1/2 cups flour
> 1 teaspoon soda
> 1 teaspoon cream of tartar
> food coloring
> Any edible decorations you want
> (sprinkles, red hots, silver balls)

Cream the butter and sugar. Add the egg and extracts. Sift flour, soda, and cream of tartar together. Add to butter mixture. Wrap dough in plastic wrap and chill overnight. Roll out and cut into desired shapes. Bake in a 350 degree oven for 10 to 12 minutes.

Icing is simply confectioner's sugar mixed with teaspoons of half and half until desired consistency is reached. To color the icing, add food coloring of choice.

SWEDISH ST. LUCY GINGER SNAPS (SWEDISH PEPPARKAKOR)

Made on St. Lucy's Day.

> 2 cups plus 1 tablespoon flour
> 2 teaspoons ground ginger
> 1 1/2 teaspoons baking soda
> 1 teaspoon ground cinnamon
> 1/2 teaspoon ground cardamom
> 1/2 teaspoon ground cloves
> 1 cup lightly packed light brown
>   sugar
> 1/4 teaspoon salt
> 10 tablespoons butter, softened
> 1/4 cup molasses
> 1 egg
> 1 teaspoon vanilla extract
> Coarse sugar, for sprinkling

In a medium bowl, combine the flour, ginger, baking soda, cinnamon, cardamom, cloves, and salt. Set aside.

In a large bowl with an electric mixer or in the bowl of a stand mixer fitted with the paddle attachment, beat the brown sugar and butter on medium speed until fluffy, about 1 minute. Add the molasses, eggs, and vanilla, and beat on medium speed until smooth, scraping the sides and bottom of the bowl with a rubber spatula as necessary.

With the mixer on low speed, gradually add the dry ingredients, beating until combined.

Divide the dough into two equal portions. Lay each portion of the dough on a piece of parchment paper generously sprinkled with flour. Sprinkle the top of the dough with more flour, and cover it with another piece of parchment paper. Roll each ball of dough out between its two pieces of parchment paper, to a thickness of 1/4 inch. Stack both pieces of rolled dough on a baking sheet, and refrigerate until firm, at least 1 hour.

Preheat the oven to 350 degrees. Prepare baking sheets by lining them with clean parchment paper or silicone baking mats.

Remove one portion of chilled dough from the refrigerator and remove the top sheet of parchment paper. Cut out the cookies using a 2- to 2 1/2-inch round cookie cutter. Using a thin spatula, gently place the cookies on the prepared baking sheets, leaving several inches between cookies. You can roll leftover dough scraps into a ball and roll them back out between floured parchment sheets as mentioned in step 4, and cut out more cookies. The dough softens very quickly and becomes hard to work with. If it gets too soft, put it back in the refrigerator until it firms up. Meanwhile, you can work with the other chilled portion of dough.

Sprinkle the cookies with the coarse sugar, and bake them for 10 minutes. When the cookies are done, they will be puffed and look dry; they will flatten as they cool.

Remove the baking sheets from the oven and allow the cookies to cool on the baking sheets for 2 to 3 minutes before placing the cookies on a cooling rack to cool completely. Store leftovers in an airtight container. I think they are crispier and taste even better on day two!

Recipe from www.fathomaway.com

TAMALES

Made on Christmas Eve and Christmas Day.

Tamale Filling:

> 1 1/4 pounds pork loin
> 1 large onion, halved
> 1 clove garlic
> 4 dried California chile pods
> 2 cups water
> 1 1/2 teaspoons salt

Tamale Dough:

> 2 cups masa harina
> 1 (10.5 ounce) can beef broth
> 1 teaspoon baking powder
> 1/2 teaspoon salt
> 2/3 cup lard
> 1 (8 ounce) package dried corn husks
> 1 cup sour cream

Place pork into a Dutch oven with onion and garlic, and add water to cover. Bring to a boil, then reduce heat to low and simmer until the meat is cooked through, about 2 hours.

Use rubber gloves to remove stems and seeds from the chile pods. Place chiles in a saucepan with 2 cups of water. Simmer, uncovered, for 20 minutes, then remove from heat to cool. Transfer the chiles and water to a blender and blend until smooth. Strain the mixture, stir in salt, and set aside. Shred the cooked meat and mix in one cup of the chile sauce.

Soak the corn husks in a bowl of warm water. In a large bowl, beat the lard with a tablespoon of the broth until fluffy. Combine the masa harina, baking powder and salt; stir into the lard mixture, adding more broth as necessary to form a spongy dough.

Spread the dough out over the corn husks to 1/4 to 1/2 inch thickness. Place one tablespoon of the meat filling into the center. Fold the sides of the husks in toward the center and place in a steamer. Steam for 1 hour.

Remove tamales from husks and drizzle remaining chile sauce over. Top with sour cream. For a creamy sauce, mix sour cream into the chile sauce.

Recipe from allrecipes.com